Music Theory for Guitar

LEVEL THREE

Amy Hite

Cover Design by Vincent Williams
Interior Layout and Graphic Design by Seth Butler

About the Author

Amy Hite is a guitar teacher and classical guitarist in Temecula, CA. Amy graduated Magna Cum Laude with a master's degree in Classical Guitar Performance from California State University, Fullerton. She held an Associate Professor of Music position at Riverside City College and served as the chair of the Guitar Syllabus Committee for the Certificate of Merit™ program with the Music Teacher's Association of California.

Amy enjoys composing and arranging music and creating comprehensive pedagogical materials for guitar students. She is also a certified yoga and Alexander Technique teacher. More about Amy can be found at www.AmyHiteGuitar.com.

About this Series

Music Theory for Guitar is a workbook series designed to help guitarists learn and practice music theory.

The workbooks include lessons and exercises covering all aspects of music theory, including music notation, rhythms, scales, intervals, key signatures, chord construction, fretboard theory, music analysis, common guitar terms, and music symbols.

Workbooks included in this series:
Music Theory for Guitar: Level 1
Music Theory for Guitar: Level 2
Music Theory for Guitar: Level 3
Music Theory for Guitar: Answer Book, Levels 1 - 3

Copyright © 2021 by Amy Hite. All rights reserved.

No part of this book may be reproduced or transmitted in any form without permission from Amy Hite.

Notes to the Student

Music theory helps you move ahead faster with your guitar playing and understanding of music. When you learn music theory along with playing the guitar, you learn to understand what you play and you will gain thorough knowledge of your instrument.

When going through this workbook, always use a pencil (not a pen!) and have an eraser close by. Take your time, read all of the instructions thoroughly, and check your answers. Have fun and enjoy the journey of learning music theory!

Notes to the Teacher

Music Theory for Guitar is a comprehensive workbook series designed to supplement music lessons. Students can be assigned one page or one chapter each week, depending on the capacity of the student.

It is suggested that you check your students' work each week and have them correct any mistakes.

This series is helpful for teachers as it can help your students learn their notes, rhythms, and other music concepts quickly so you don't have to review the same material over and over with them during their lessons.

The workbooks are valuable for guitar students learning any style at any age. They can be used in preparation for auditions to music academies or schools, or for theory tests given in music certificate programs. Teachers may find it helpful to reference the answer book for this series when correcting their students' homework.

MUSIC THEORY FOR GUITAR: LEVEL 3
TABLE OF CONTENTS

Chapter 1: Notes on the Fretboard 5

Chapter 2: Major Key Signatures 16

Chapter 3: Major Scales 23

Chapter 4: Minor Key Signatures 27

Chapter 5: Minor Scales 31

Chapter 6: Intervals 39

Chapter 7: The Circle of 5ths.. 45

Chapter 8: Triads 51

Chapter 9: Chords 55

Chapter 10: Barre Chords 63

Chapter 11: Cadences 71

Chapter 12: Chord Progressions 76

Chapter 13: Transposition 85

Chapter 14: Rhythms 91

Chapter 15: Dotted Rhythms 95

Chapter 16: Rests 98

Chapter 17: Time Signatures 102

Chapter 18: Signs and Terms 110

Chapter 19: Music Analysis 114

Final Exam 116

CHAPTER 1

Notes on the Fretboard

Here are all the notes on the guitar up to the twelfth fret.

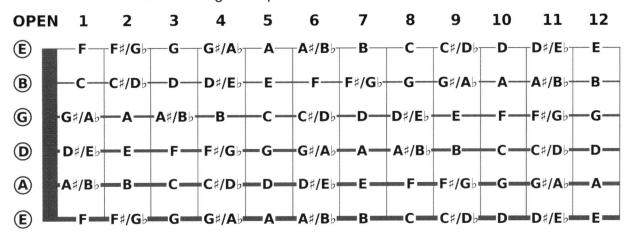

Notice that all of the natural notes have sharps and flats between them except for B and C, and E and F. This is because B and C are a half step apart and E and F are a half step apart. All other pairs of natural notes are a whole step apart.

Remembering that half steps lie between notes E and F and notes B and C, we can count up from each open string to find the rest of the notes on that string.

Here are all the notes on the **first string** through the twelfth fret. The Roman numerals under the fretboard represent fret numbers. Notice that all natural notes are a whole step apart except for the Es and Fs and the Bs and Cs.

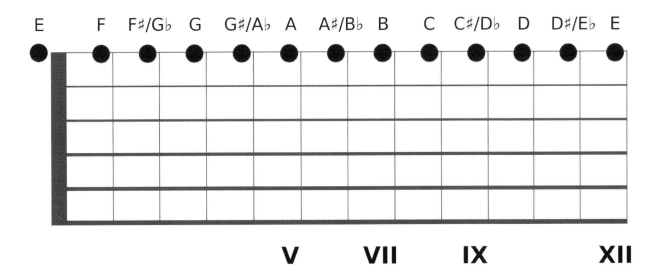

5

1. Write the names of the notes on the **second string**.

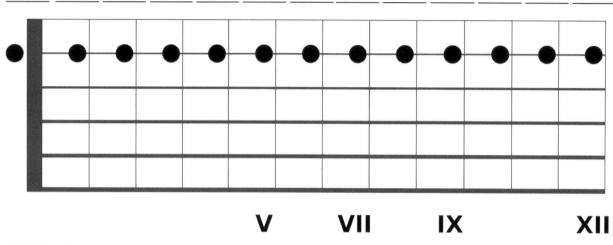

2. Write the names of the notes on the **third string**.

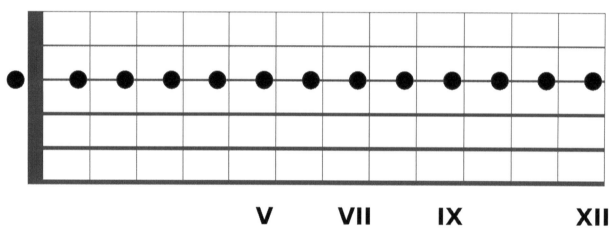

3. Write the names of the notes on the **fourth string**.

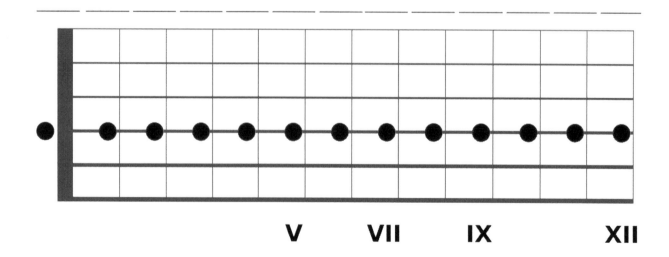

4. Write the names of the notes on the **fifth string**.

___ ___ ___ ___ ___ ___ ___ ___ ___ ___ ___ ___ ___

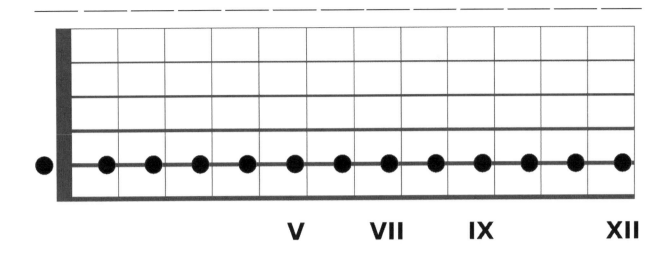

5. Write the names of the notes on the **sixth string**.

___ ___ ___ ___ ___ ___ ___ ___ ___ ___ ___ ___ ___

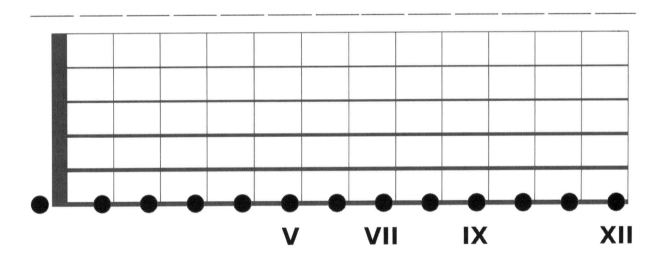

Here are some tips for finding notes on the fretboard:

Tip #1 - Every twelfth fret note is one octave above the open string. For example, the open first string is E and the twelfth fret of the first string is also E.

7

6. Fill in the blanks. The first one is done for you.

　　　　Open 6th string is _E_ , so the 12th fret of the 6th string is also _E_ .

　　　　Open 5th string is ___ , so the 12th fret of the 5th string is also ___ .

　　　　Open 4th string is ___ , so the 12th fret of the 4th string is also ___ .

　　　　Open 3rd string is ___ , so the 12th fret of the 3rd string is also ___ .

　　　　Open 2nd string is ___ , so the 12th fret of the 2nd string is also ___ .

　　　　Open 1st string is ___ , so the 12th fret of the 1st string is also ___ .

Tip #2 - To find the name of a note on a higher fret, it may be easier to count backwards from the twelfth fret. For example, the tenth fret notes are a whole step below the twelfth fret.

7. Fill in the blanks. Count a whole step backwards from the twelfth fret to find the tenth fret notes on each string. The first one is done for you.

　　　　Fret 12 of string 6 is _E_ . Fret 10 of string 6 is _D_ .

　　　　Fret 12 of string 5 is ___ . Fret 10 of string 5 is ___ .

　　　　Fret 12 of string 4 is ___ . Fret 10 of string 4 is ___ .

　　　　Fret 12 of string 3 is ___ . Fret 10 of string 3 is ___ .

　　　　Fret 12 of string 2 is ___ . Fret 10 of string 2 is ___ .

　　　　Fret 12 of string 1 is ___ . Fret 10 of string 1 is ___ .

Tip #3 - As the open first string and open sixth string are both E, every fret of these strings are the same note name. For example, the seventh fret of string one is B and the seventh fret of string six is also B.

8. Write the fret number for each note as it lies on BOTH E strings (string 1 and string 6). The first one is done for you.

Fret: _4_   ___   ___   ___   ___   ___   ___   ___   ___   ___   ___

Note: G♯   F   D♯   A   B♭   C♯   D   F♯   C   G   B

Tip #4 - All of the fifth fret notes are the same note as the open string **underneath** it except for the third string, where it lies on the fourth fret (fourth fret of third string is B as the open second string is B).

Example: The open fourth string is D, so the fifth fret of the fifth string is also D.

9. Use tip #4 to name the notes. The first one is done for you.

     5th fret 6th string: _A_

     5th fret 5th string: ___

     5th fret 4th string: ___

     4th fret 3rd string: ___

     5th fret 2nd string: ___

Tip #5 (last one!) - All of the seventh fret notes have the same note name as the open string **above** it except for the second string, where it lies on the eighth fret (eighth fret of second string is G as the open third string is G).

Example: The open sixth string is E, so the seventh fret of the fifth string is also E.

10. Use tip #5 to name the notes.

     7th fret 1st string: ___

     8th fret 2nd string: ___

     7th fret 3rd string: ___

     7th fret 4th string: ___

     7th fret 5th string: ___

11. Use tips 1 through 5 to name the notes on the fretboard images below. This is a lot to remember, but the more you practice, the easier it gets!

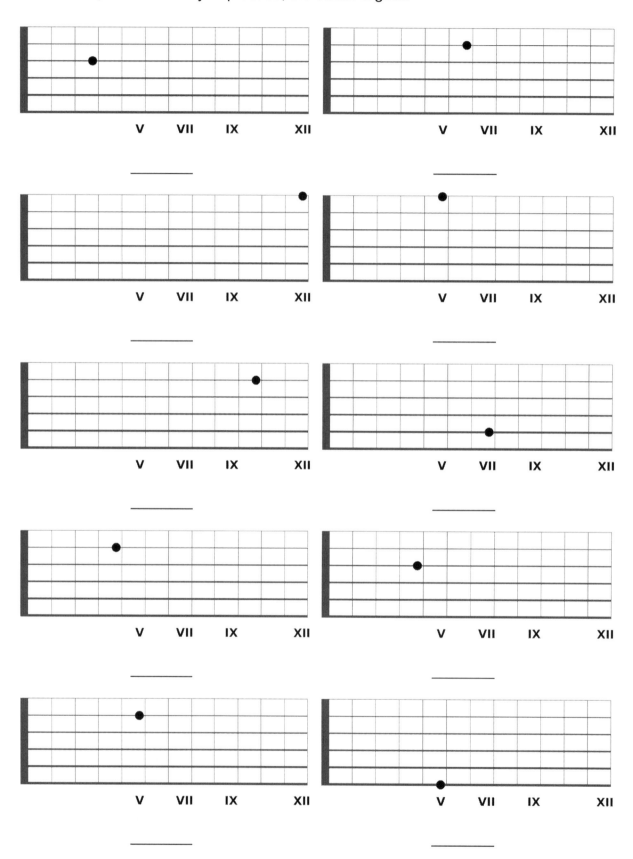

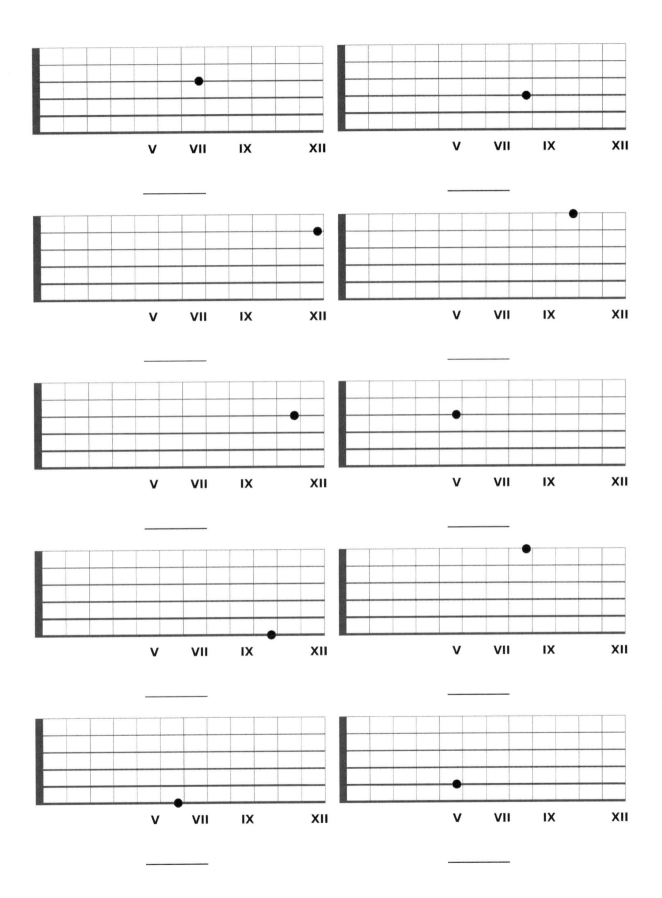

12. Write the fret number where each note can be found on each string. The first one is done for you.

Note: E

String number	Fret number
1	_12_
3	____
5	____
4	____
6	____
2	____

Note: C

String number	Fret number
2	____
4	____
1	____
3	____
5	____
6	____

Note: B

String number	Fret number
6	____
3	____
5	____
1	____
4	____
2	____

Note: A

String number	Fret number
3	____
1	____
6	____
5	____
4	____
2	____

Note: G

String number	Fret number
2	____
1	____
3	____
4	____
6	____
5	____

Note: F

String number	Fret number
1	____
2	____
6	____
5	____
4	____
3	____

Note: D

String number	Fret number
6	____
5	____
4	____
3	____
1	____
2	____

FRETBOARD NOTES ON THE STAFF

Here are all the notes on each string, open through the twelfth fret, as written on the music staff.

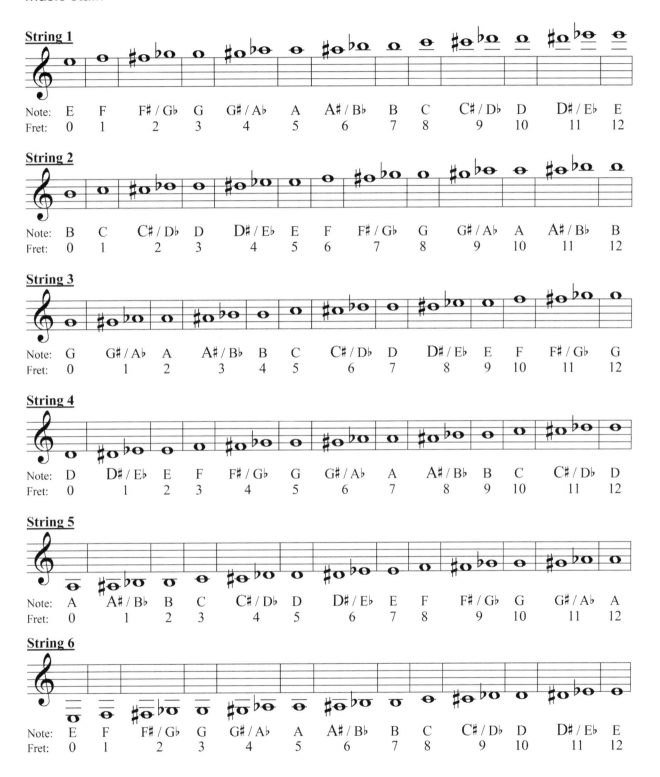

13. Write the note name and fret number under each note. The first one is done for you.

Notes on the **first string**

Note: E ___ ___ ___ ___ ___ ___ ___ ___ ___
Fret: 0 ___ ___ ___ ___ ___ ___ ___ ___ ___

Note: ___ ___ ___ ___ ___ ___ ___ ___ ___ ___
Fret: ___ ___ ___ ___ ___ ___ ___ ___ ___ ___

Notes on the **second string**

Note: ___ ___ ___ ___ ___ ___ ___ ___ ___ ___
Fret: ___ ___ ___ ___ ___ ___ ___ ___ ___ ___

Note: ___ ___ ___ ___ ___ ___ ___ ___ ___ ___
Fret: ___ ___ ___ ___ ___ ___ ___ ___ ___ ___

Notes on the **third string**

Note: ___ ___ ___ ___ ___ ___ ___ ___ ___ ___
Fret: ___ ___ ___ ___ ___ ___ ___ ___ ___ ___

Note: ___ ___ ___ ___ ___ ___ ___ ___ ___ ___
Fret: ___ ___ ___ ___ ___ ___ ___ ___ ___ ___

Notes on the **fourth string**

Note: ____ ____ ____ ____ ____ ____ ____ ____ ____ ____
Fret: ____ ____ ____ ____ ____ ____ ____ ____ ____ ____

Note: ____ ____ ____ ____ ____ ____ ____ ____ ____ ____
Fret: ____ ____ ____ ____ ____ ____ ____ ____ ____ ____

Notes on the **fifth string**

Note: ____ ____ ____ ____ ____ ____ ____ ____ ____ ____
Fret: ____ ____ ____ ____ ____ ____ ____ ____ ____ ____

Note: ____ ____ ____ ____ ____ ____ ____ ____ ____ ____
Fret: ____ ____ ____ ____ ____ ____ ____ ____ ____ ____

Notes on the **sixth string**

Note: ____ ____ ____ ____ ____ ____ ____ ____ ____ ____
Fret: ____ ____ ____ ____ ____ ____ ____ ____ ____ ____

Note: ____ ____ ____ ____ ____ ____ ____ ____ ____ ____
Fret: ____ ____ ____ ____ ____ ____ ____ ____ ____ ____

CHAPTER 2

Major Key Signatures

A key signature tells us the key that a song is written in. It can be found to the right of the treble clef at the beginning of a song.

If a key signature has sharps or flats, the sharp or flat signs will be written next to the treble clef. All notes with the same note name on which the sharp or flat signs are written will be played sharp or flat throughout the song.

Example: In the line below, as the key signature has an F sharp, **all** of the Fs are played sharp.

THE ORDER OF SHARPS

Sharp signs always appear in the same order. This is the order of sharps:

      F   C   G   D   A   E   B

This means that if a key signature has one sharp, that sharp will be F.
If a key signature has two sharps, they will be F and C.
If a key signature has three sharps, they will be F, C, and G, and so on.

This is the way the order of sharps appears on the staff. Notice that the G is the highest sharp and the A is the lowest sharp.

 An easy way to learn the order of sharps is to remember the sentence **F**at **C**ats **G**o **D**own **A**lleys **E**ating **B**irds.

16

1. Draw the order of sharps four times as it is shown in the example on the previous page.

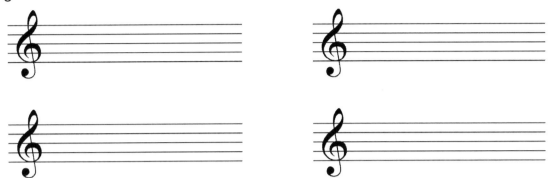

2. Fill in the blanks. Always name the sharps in order beginning with F. The first one is done for you.

a. If a key signature has 4 sharps, they will be _F_, _C_, _G_, and _D_.

b. If a key signature has 6 sharps, they will be ___, ___, ___, ___, ___, and ___.

c. If a key signature has 2 sharps, they will be ___ and ___.

d. If a key signature has 5 sharps, they will be ___, ___, ___, ___, and ___.

e. If a key signature has 1 sharp, it will be ___.

f. If a key signature has 3 sharps, they will be ___, ___, and ___.

g. If a key signature has 7 sharps, they will be ___, ___, ___, ___, ___, ___, and ___.

THE ORDER OF FLATS

Key signatures can have sharps OR flats. This is the order of flats:

    B   E   A   D   G   C   F

This means that if a key signature has one flat, that flat will be B.
If a key signature has two flats, they will be B and E, and so on.

This is the way the order of flats appears on the staff. Notice that the E is the highest flat and the F is the lowest flat.

An easy way to learn the order of flats is to remember the saying **BEAD G**um **C**andy **F**ruit.

3. Draw the order of flats four times as it is shown in the example on the previous page.

4. Fill in the blanks. Always name the flats in order beginning with B. The first one is done for you.

a. If a key signature has 4 flats, they will be _B_, _E_, _A_, and _D_.

b. If a key signature has 1 flat, it will be ___.

c. If a key signature has 2 flats, they will be ___ and ___.

d. If a key signature has 5 flats, they will be ___, ___, ___, ___, and ___.

e. If a key signature has 6 flats, they will be ___, ___, ___, ___, ___, and ___.

f. If a key signature has 3 flats, they will be ___, ___, and ___.

g. if a key signature has 7 flats, they will be ___, ___, ___, ___, ___, ___, and ___.

MAJOR KEY SIGNATURES

The key signature with no sharps or flats is C Major. This should be memorized.

To name the Major key for a key signature that has sharps, go up one half step above the last sharp (the sharp farthest to the right on the staff).

Example:

The last sharp in this key signature is G♯. One half step above G♯ is A, so this is the key of A Major.

5. Fill in the blanks to determine the Major key signatures. Always name the sharps in order. The first one is done for you.

The sharps in this key signature are _F_, _C_, _G_, _D_, _A_, _E_, and _B_. The last sharp is _B♯_. A half step above _B♯_ is _C♯_. This is the key of _C♯_ Major.

The sharps in this key signature are ___, ___, ___, ___, ___, and ___. The last sharp is ___. A half step above ___ is ___. This is the key of ___ Major.

The sharps in this key signature are ___ and ___. The last sharp is ___. A half step above ___ is ___. This is the key of ___ Major.

The sharps in this key signature are ___, ___, ___, and ___. The last sharp is ___. A half step above ___ is ___. This is the key of ___ Major.

The sharp in this key signature is ___. A half step above ___ is ___. This is the key of ___ Major.

The sharps in this key signature are ___, ___, ___, ___, and ___. The last sharp is ___. A half step above ___ is ___. This is the key of ___ Major.

The sharps in this key signature are ___, ___, and ___. The last sharp is ___. A half step above ___ is ___. This is the key of ___ Major.

The name of the Major key for key signatures with flats is the name of the second to last flat.

Example:

The second to last flat in this key signature is D♭, so this is the key of D♭ Major.

The key signature with one flat should be memorized. This is the key of F Major.

6. Fill in the blanks to determine the Major key signatures. Always name the flats in order. The first one is done for you.

The flats in this key signature are _B_, _E_, _A_, and _D_. The second to last flat is _A♭_. This is the key of _A♭_ Major.

The flats in this key signature are ___, ___, and ___. The second to last flat is ___. This is the key of ___ Major.

The flats in this key signature are ___ and ___. The second to last flat is ___. This is the key of ___ Major.

The flats in this key signature are ___, ___, ___, ___, ___, and ___. The second to last flat is ___. This is the key of ___ Major.

The flats in this key signature are ___, ___, ___, ___, and ___. The second to last flat is ___. This is the key of ___ Major.

 This is the key of ___ Major.

 The flats in this key signature are ___, ___, ___, ___, ___, ___, and ___. The second to last flat is ___. This is the key of ___ Major.

NAMING ALL MAJOR KEY SIGNATURES

7. Name the Major key for each key signature.

 _____ Major

 _____ Major

 _____ Major

 _____ Major

 _____ Major

 _____ Major

 _____ Major

 _____ Major

 _____ Major

 _____ Major

 _____ Major

 _____ Major

 _____ Major

8. Draw the key signatures.

Sharp keys:

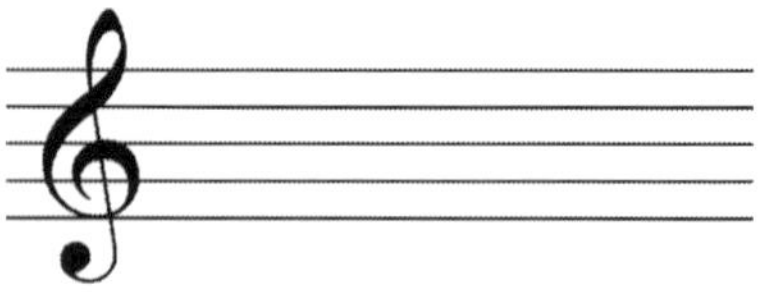

F♯ Major

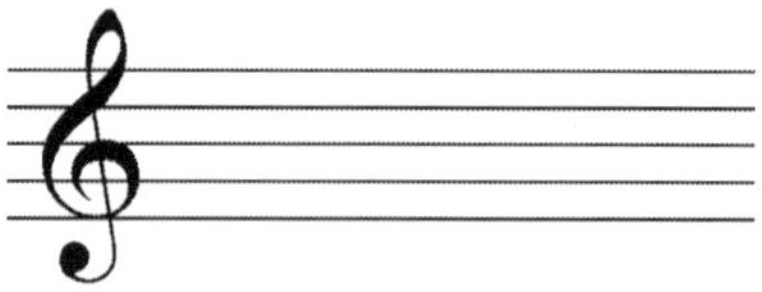

E Major

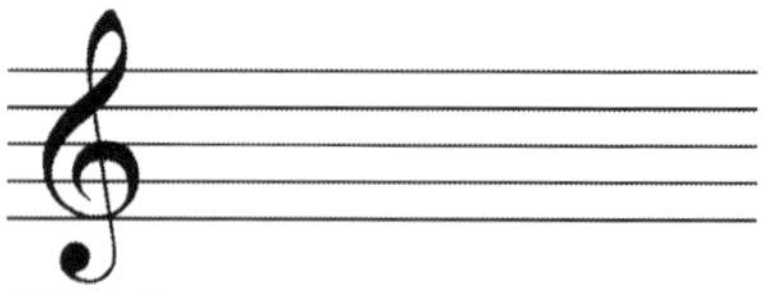

G Major

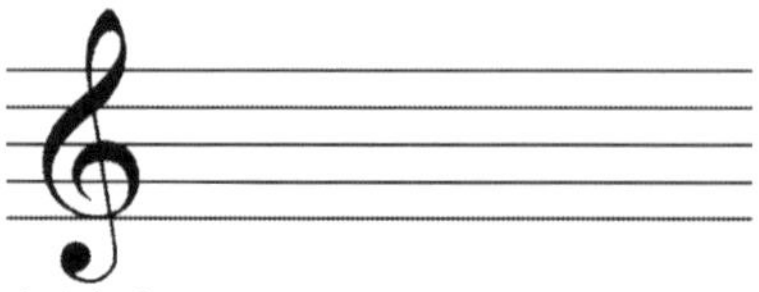

A Major

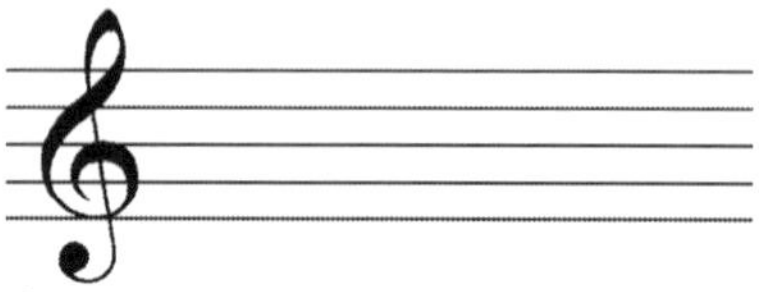

C Major

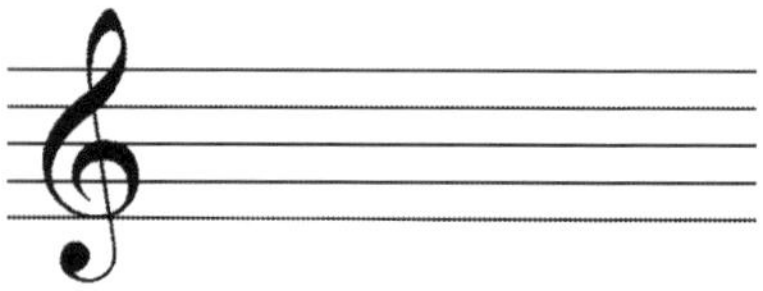

D Major

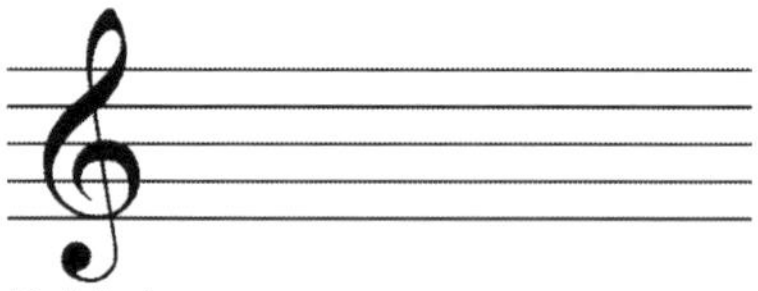

B Major

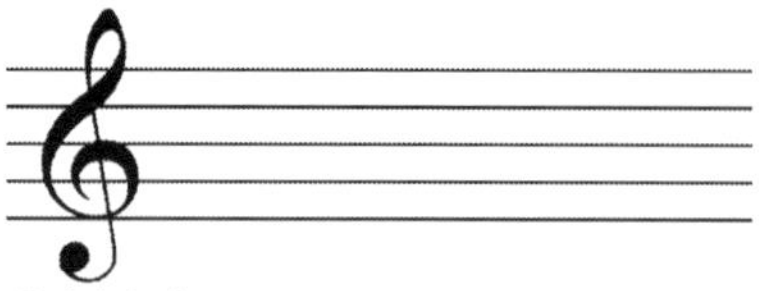

C♯ Major

Flat keys:

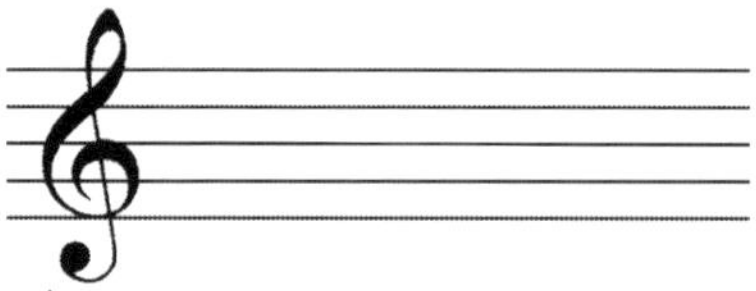

B♭ Major

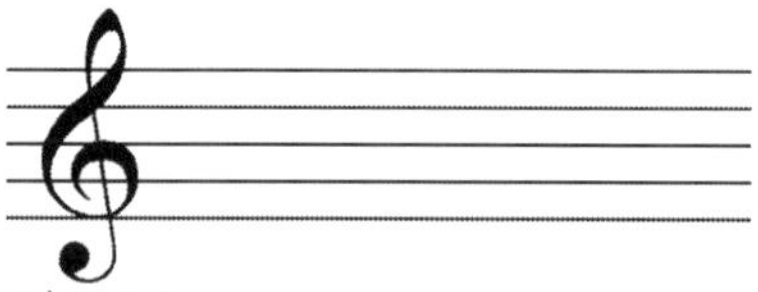

A♭ Major

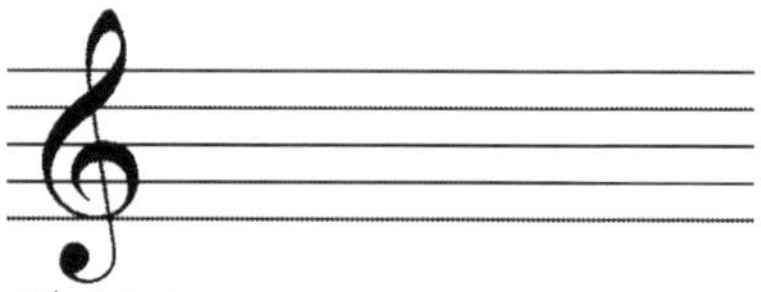

G♭ Major

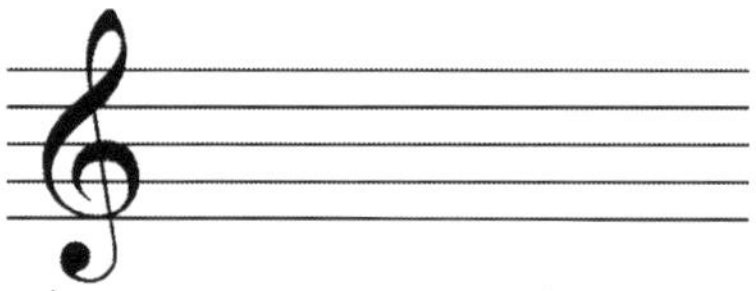

C♭ Major

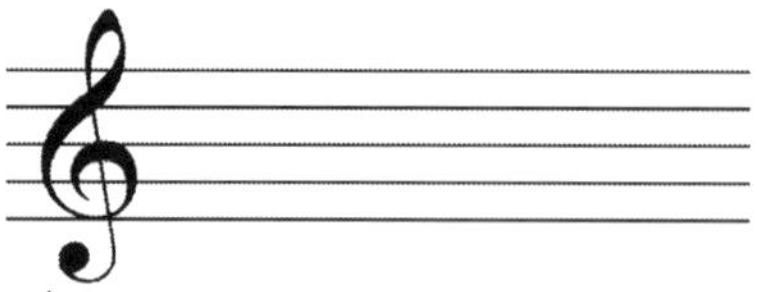

E♭ Major

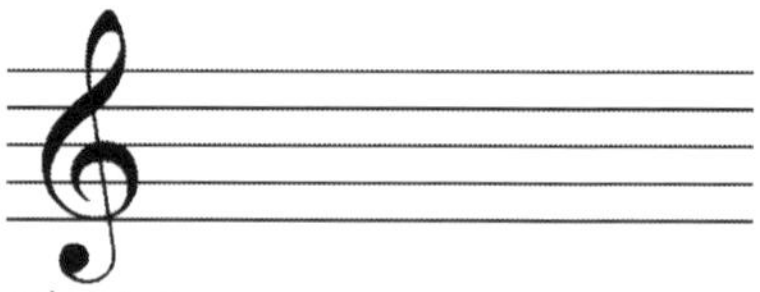

D♭ Major

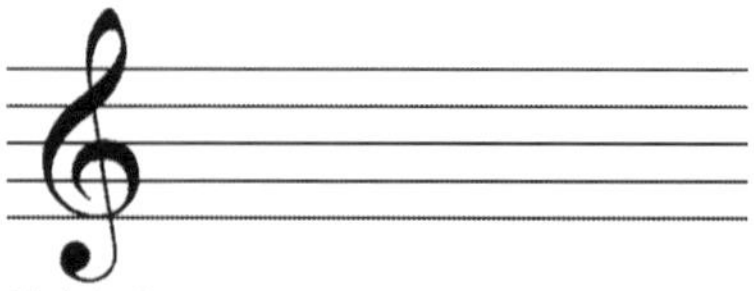

F Major

CHAPTER 3

Major Scales

Major scales have eight notes. They begin and end on the note for which the scale is named; for example, the G Major scale begins and ends on G. The notes of each Major scale contain the same notes as the Major key signature.

Examples:

This is a G Major scale. Just the like the G Major key signature, the G Major scale has one sharp, which is F♯.

This is an E Major scale. Just like the E Major key signature, the E Major scale has four sharps, which are F♯, C♯, G♯, and D♯.

1. Add **sharps** to complete the Major scales. Draw the sharp signs to the left of the notes when needed and draw them on the same line or space on which the notes lie.

D Major:

G Major:

F♯ Major:

C Major:

A Major:

C♯ Major:

B Major:

E Major:

23

2. Add **flats** to complete the Major scales. Draw the flat signs to the left of the notes when needed and draw them on the same line or space on which the notes lie.

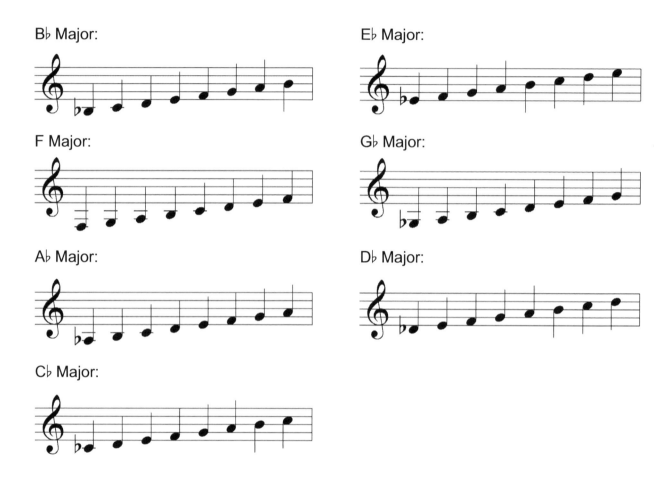

Here is a completely different way to form a Major scale - Begin with the first note and count the following pattern of whole steps and half steps:

Whole - Whole - Half - Whole - Whole - Whole - Half

Example: This is an E♭ Major scale. Notice that the notes follow the whole step and half step pattern above so that the distance between E♭ to F is a whole step, the distance from F to G is a whole step, the distance from G to A♭ is a half step, and so on.

3. Use the whole step and half step pattern to complete the Major scales. Draw **quarter notes**. Draw sharp or flat signs to the left of the notes when needed. The first example is done for you.

Scales with <u>sharps</u>:

Scales with **flats**:

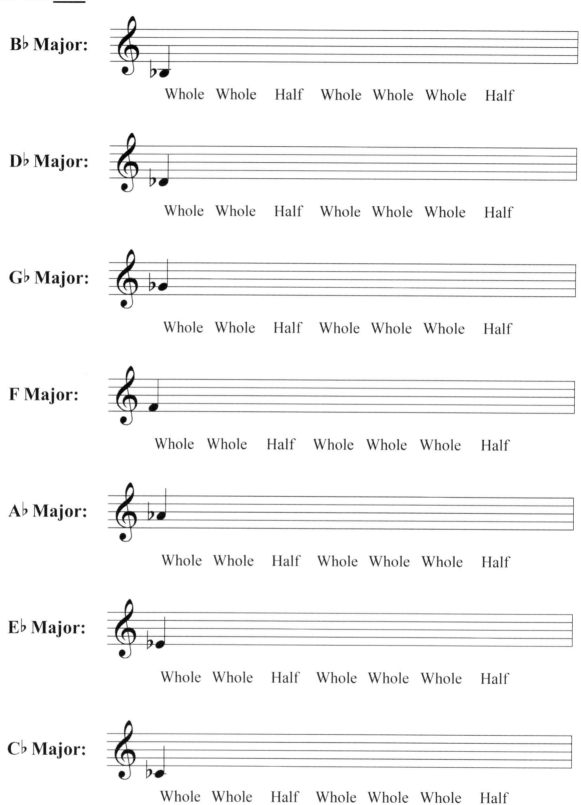

26

CHAPTER 4
Minor Key Signatures

RELATIVE MAJOR AND MINOR

Every Major key has a **relative minor** key that shares the same key signature. The name of the relative minor key is the sixth note of the Major scale.

Example: The sixth note of the B Major scale is G♯, so the relative minor key to B Major is g♯ minor.

B Major scale:

B	C♯	D♯	E	F♯	G♯	A♯	B	relative minor: g♯ minor
1	2	3	4	5	6	7	8	

 This is the key signature for B Major and g♯ minor.

1. Write the notes of the following **Major scales**. Then name the **relative minor key**, which is the sixth note of the Major scale. Notice that minor keys are written as lowercase letters whereas Major keys are written as uppercase letters. The first one is done for you.

Scales with **sharps**:

E Major scale:

E	F♯	G♯	A	B	C♯	D♯	E	relative minor: __c♯__ minor
1	2	3	4	5	6	7	8	

G Major scale:

___ ___ ___ ___ ___ ___ ___ ___   relative minor: ____ minor
1   2   3   4   5   6   7   8

A Major scale:

___ ___ ___ ___ ___ ___ ___ ___   relative minor: ____ minor
1   2   3   4   5   6   7   8

27

B Major scale:

___ ___ ___ ___ ___ ___ ___ ___   relative minor: ___ minor
 1   2   3   4   5   6   7   8

F♯ Major scale:

___ ___ ___ ___ ___ ___ ___ ___   relative minor: ___ minor
 1   2   3   4   5   6   7   8

D Major scale:

___ ___ ___ ___ ___ ___ ___ ___   relative minor: ___ minor
 1   2   3   4   5   6   7   8

C Major scale:

___ ___ ___ ___ ___ ___ ___ ___   relative minor: ___ minor
 1   2   3   4   5   6   7   8

Scales with **flats**:

F Major scale:

___ ___ ___ ___ ___ ___ ___ ___   relative minor: ___ minor
 1   2   3   4   5   6   7   8

A♭ Major scale:

___ ___ ___ ___ ___ ___ ___ ___   relative minor: ___ minor
 1   2   3   4   5   6   7   8

G♭ Major scale:

___ ___ ___ ___ ___ ___ ___ ___   relative minor: ___ minor
 1   2   3   4   5   6   7   8

E♭ Major scale:

___ ___ ___ ___ ___ ___ ___ ___   relative minor: ___ minor
 1   2   3   4   5   6   7   8

D♭ Major scale:

___ ___ ___ ___ ___ ___ ___ ___   relative minor: ___ minor
 1   2   3   4   5   6   7   8

B♭ Major scale:

___ ___ ___ ___ ___ ___ ___ ___   relative minor: ___ minor
 1   2   3   4   5   6   7   8

2. Name the following key signatures, both Major and minor. The first one is done for you.

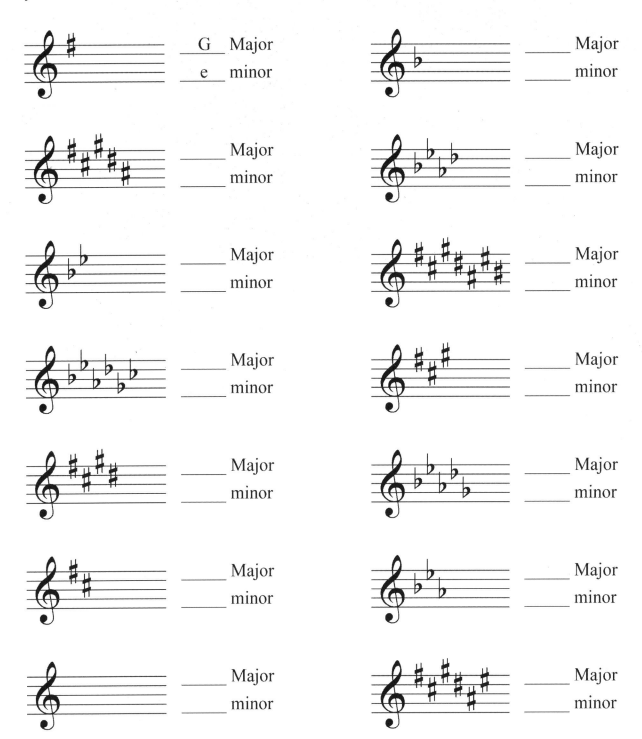

3. Draw the following minor key signatures.

Sharp keys:

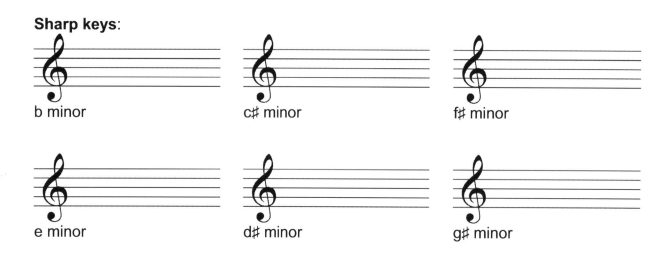

Flat keys:

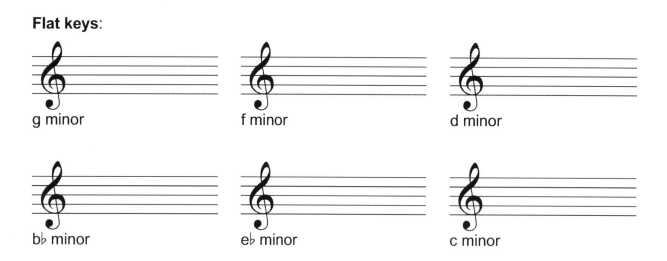

CHAPTER 5

Minor Scales

The Three Types of Minor Scales	
Natural minor scale	Contains all notes within the key signature
Harmonic minor scale	The seventh note is raised a half step
Melodic minor scale	The sixth and seventh notes are raised a half step on the ascending scale, returns to natural minor on descending scale

NATURAL MINOR SCALES

Natural minor scales have the same notes that are in the key signature.
Examples:
This is an a natural minor scale. As the a minor key signature has no sharps or flats, the a natural minor scale also has no sharps or flats.

This is a g natural minor scale. As the g minor key signature has B♭ and E♭, the g natural minor scale also has B♭ and E♭.

1. Add **sharps** to complete the natural minor scales. Draw the sharp signs to the left of the notes when needed and draw them on the same line or space on which the notes lie.

e natural minor   b natural minor

31

2. Add **flats** to complete the natural minor scales. Draw the flat signs to the left of the notes when needed and draw them on the same line or space on which the notes lie.

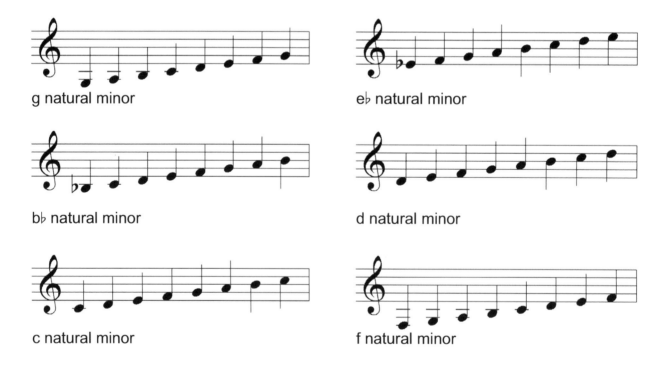

32

Here is a completely different way to form a natural minor scale: Begin with the first note and count the following pattern of whole steps and half steps:

Whole - Half - Whole - Whole - Half - Whole - Whole

Example: This is an f♯ natural minor scale. Notice that the notes follow the whole step and half step pattern above.

3. Use the whole step and half step pattern above to complete the **natural minor scales**. Draw **whole notes**. Draw sharp or flat signs to the left of the notes when needed.

Scales with <u>sharps</u>:

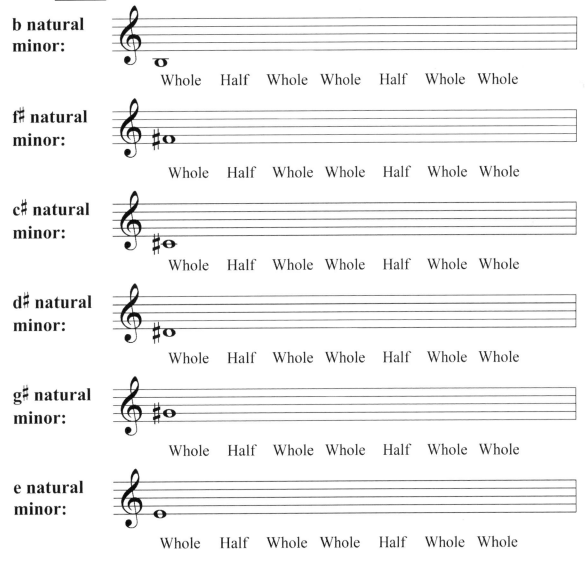

Scales with **flats**:

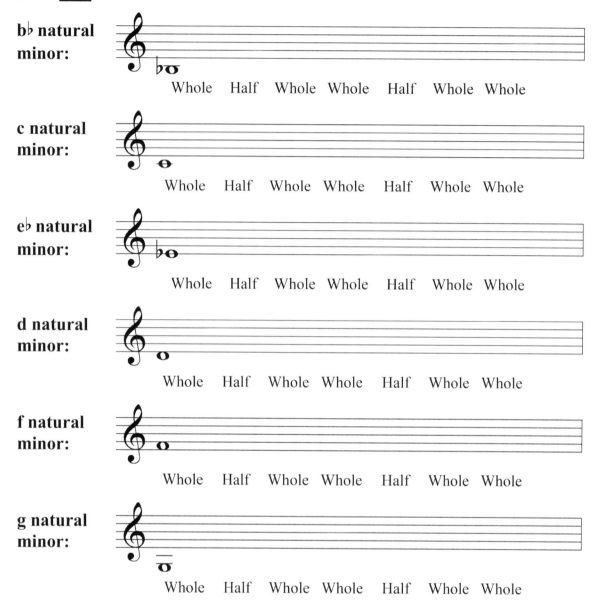

HARMONIC MINOR SCALES

The **harmonic minor scale** raises the seventh note of the natural minor scale one half step.

Example: In the a harmonic minor scale, the seventh note, which is G, is raised a half step, making it G sharp.

When the seventh note of the scale is already a sharp, that note becomes double sharp when it is raised, which is written with the following symbol:

 This is the symbol for the double sharp. As an F♯ is played on the fourth fret of the fourth string, the F double sharp can either be played on the fifth fret of the fourth string or as an open third string.

Here is an example of a g♯ harmonic minor scale with the seventh note raised as a double sharp.

When the seventh note of a scale is flat, when we raise it a half step it becomes natural.

Here is an example of a b♭ harmonic minor scale. As the A note is flat in the b♭ natural minor scale, the A is natural in the b♭ harmonic minor scale.

4. Draw the following **harmonic minor scales**. Draw **whole notes**. The first note of each scale is done for you.

35

MELODIC MINOR SCALES

The **melodic minor scale** raises the sixth and seventh notes of the natural minor scale one half step in the ascending scale (the way up the scale) and returns back to the natural minor scale in the descending scale (the way down the scale). So, it is different on the way up than on the way down.

Example:
In the a melodic minor scale, the F and G are sharp in the ascending scale and all notes are natural in the descending scale.

5. Add sharp, flat, and natural signs to complete the **melodic minor scales**. Write the scales in both directions, ascending and descending. The first one is done for you. Notice that if sharp or flat signs are included in the ascending scale, they do not need to be written again when they remain the same in the descending scale.

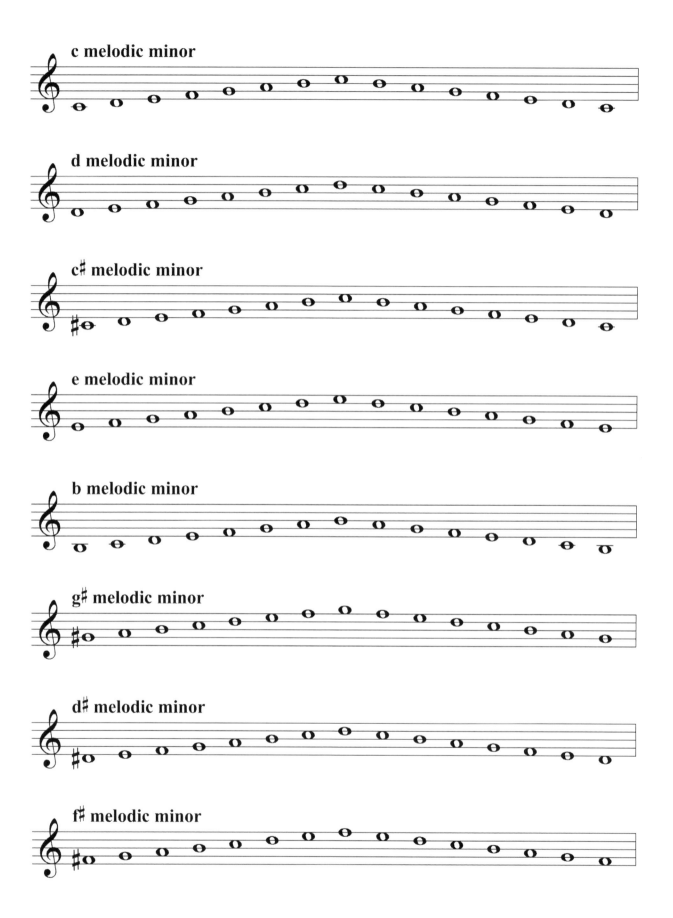

CHAPTER 6

Intervals

An **interval** is the distance between two notes. The bottom note is counted as one. Count up to the number of the second note to determine the number of the interval.

If we have two of the same notes, the interval is called a **unison**.

Unison

The interval of an eighth has two notes with the same note name. This is called an **octave**.

Octave

Intervals can either be stacked on top of each other, which we call a **harmonic** interval, or next to each other, which we call a **melodic** interval.

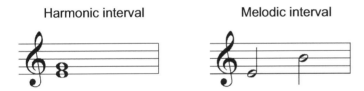

Here are examples of all intervals up to an octave.

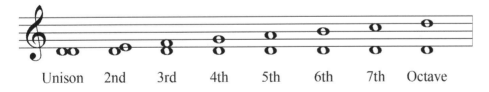

1. Number the following intervals. The first one is done for you.

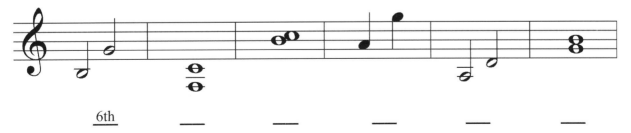

39

2. Draw the **upper** notes to complete the following intervals. Draw **whole notes** to create harmonic intervals. The first one is done for you.

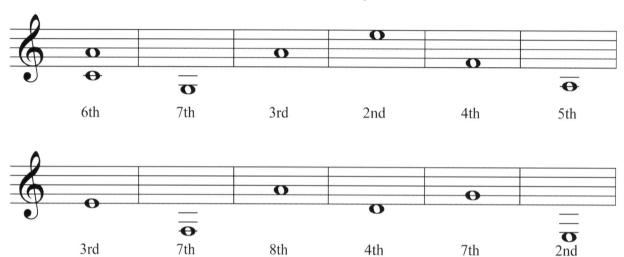

3. Draw the **lower** notes to complete the following intervals. Draw **half notes** to create melodic intervals. The first one is done for you.

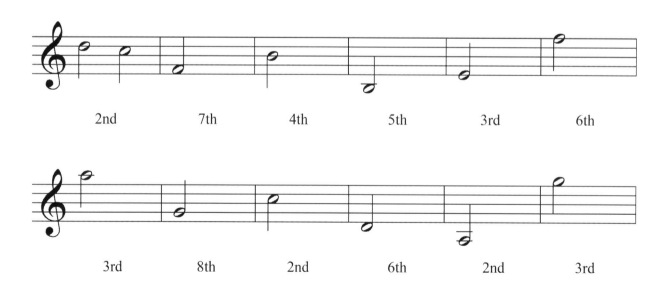

MAJOR AND PERFECT INTERVALS

If the top note of the interval is in the Major key of the bottom note, the interval is **Major** or **Perfect**. Unisons, 4ths, 5ths, and octaves (8ths) are called Perfect and 2nds, 3rds, 6ths, and 7ths are called Major.

Perfect intervals = Unisons, 4ths, 5ths, or 8ths

Major intervals = 2nds, 3rds, 6ths, or 7ths

Here are examples of Major and Perfect intervals in the key of G Major. Notice that all of the top notes are in the key of G, which is why the F is sharp.

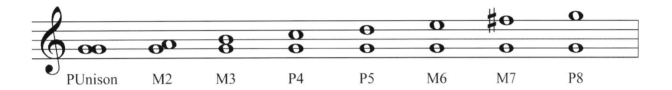

4. Name the intervals below using capital **P** for Perfect and capital **M** for Major. For example, label a Perfect 4th P4 and a Major 7th M7. The first one is done for you.

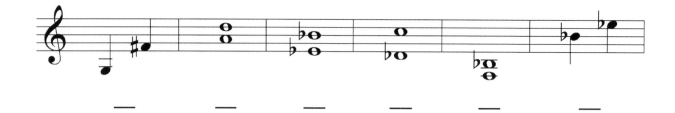

5. Draw the **upper** notes to create the following intervals and add sharp or flat signs when needed. Draw **whole notes**.

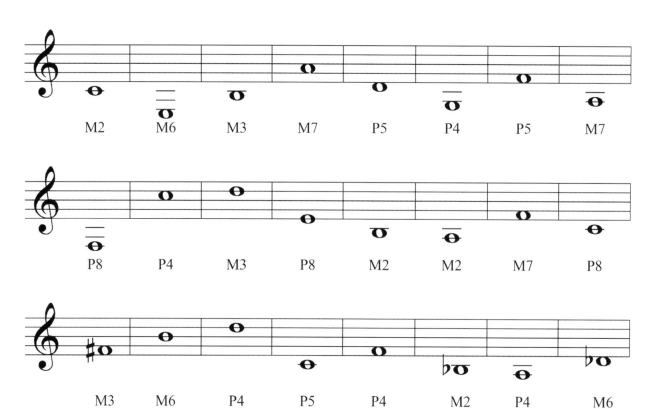

6. Name each circled interval in the music example. Notice the key signature. The first one is done for you.

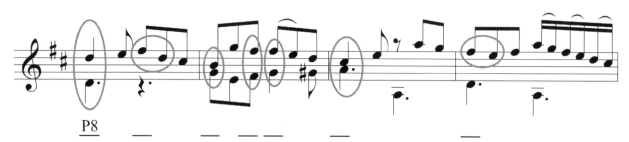

MINOR INTERVALS

Minor intervals are created by lowering the top note of a Major interval by a half step.

Here are some examples of how Major intervals become minor intervals. Notice that minor intervals are labeled with a lowercase m.

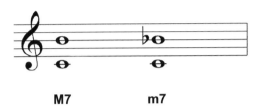

The B is lowered a half step, making it B flat.

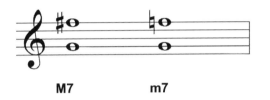

The F♯ is lowered a half step, making it F natural.

When a flat is lowered a half step, the note becomes double flat.

This is the symbol for the double flat. As a B♭ is played on the first fret of the fifth string, the B double flat is played on the open fifth string.

Here is an example of an interval with a double flat:

m6

43

7. Draw the **upper** note to create **minor** intervals. Draw all **whole notes** to create harmonic intervals and include sharp or flat signs when needed. The first one is done for you.

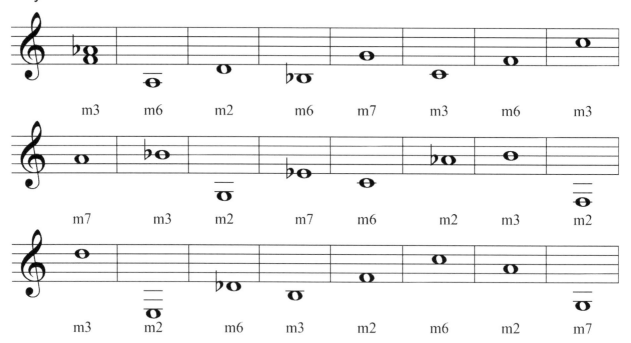

8. Name the following intervals. They can be Perfect, Major, or minor. Use capital **P** for Perfect, capital **M** for Major, and lowercase **m** for minor (for example, P5, M3, m7). The first one is done for you.

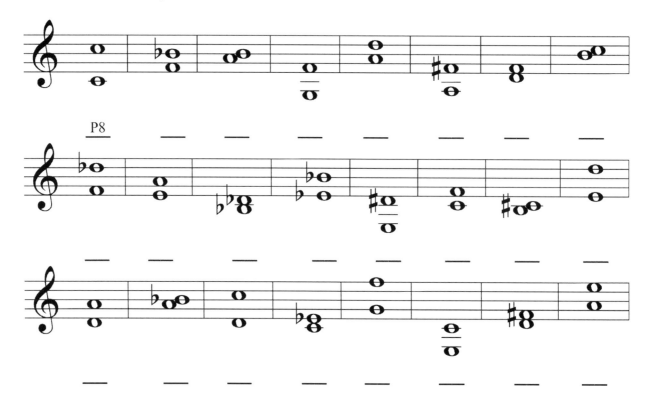

CHAPTER 7

The Circle of 5ths

The **circle of fifths** is a useful way of organizing all Major and minor key signatures, the order or sharps, and the order of flats.

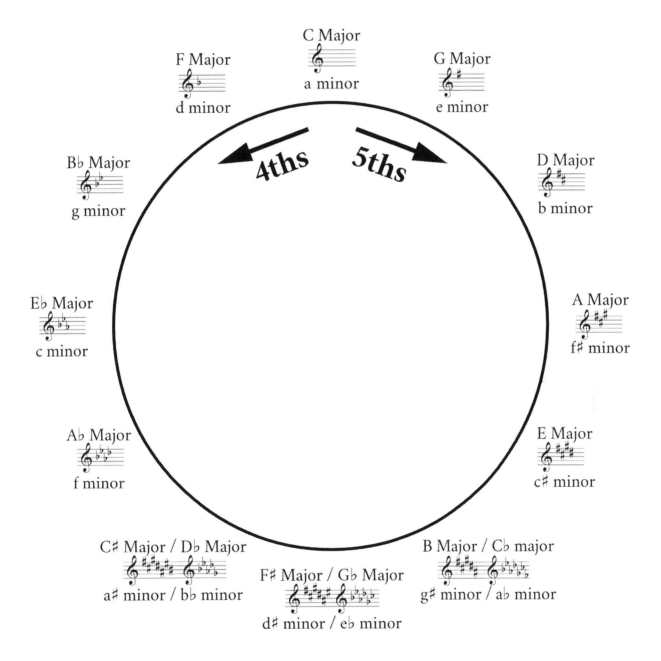

The circle of fifths contains all Major and minor keys with the sharp keys on the right side of the circle and the flat keys on the left side.

45

KEYS WITH SHARPS

The top of the circle is the key with no sharps or flats, which is C Major.

The next key to the right is the key that is an interval of a fifth above C Major, which is G Major.

The keys move around the circle in order of fifths, adding sharps along the way so that the next key (G Major) has 1 sharp, the next key (D Major) has 2 sharps, and so on. So, the order of sharp keys moves in fifths.

Example: C Major to G Major is a fifth, G Major to D Major is a fifth, and so on, all the way up to the key of C♯ Major!

$$C \xrightarrow{5th} G \xrightarrow{5th} D$$

1. Fill in the blanks to name the Major keys that have sharps as they move around the circle of fifths beginning with C Major. The fifth of one key is the next key in the circle. The first one is done for you.

No sharps:	key of _C_ Major	A fifth above _C_ is _G_ .
1 sharp:	key of _G_ Major	A fifth above _G_ is ___ .
2 sharps:	key of ___ Major	A fifth above ___ is ___ .
3 sharps:	key of ___ Major	A fifth above ___ is ___ .
4 sharps:	key of ___ Major	A fifth above ___ is ___ .
5 sharps:	key of ___ Major	A fifth above ___ is ___ .
6 sharps:	key of ___ Major	A fifth above ___ is ___ .
7 sharps:	key of ___ Major	

The minor keys with sharps also move in fifths.

Example: a minor to e minor is a fifth, e minor to b minor is a fifth, and so on.

$$a \xrightarrow{5th} e \xrightarrow{5th} b$$

2. Fill in the blanks to name the minor keys that have sharps as they move around the circle of fifths beginning with a minor. The fifth of one key is the next key in the circle. The first one is done for you.

    No sharps: key of _a_ minor   A fifth above _a_ is _e_.
    1 sharp: key of _e_ minor   A fifth above _e_ is ___.
    2 sharps: key of ___ minor   A fifth above ___ is ___.
    3 sharps: key of ___ minor   A fifth above ___ is ___.
    4 sharps: key of ___ minor   A fifth above ___ is ___.
    5 sharps: key of ___ minor   A fifth above ___ is ___.
    6 sharps: key of ___ minor   A fifth above ___ is ___.
    7 sharps: key of ___ minor

THE ORDER OF SHARPS

Just as the order of keys with sharps moves in fifths, the order of sharps also moves in fifths!

Example: The first sharp in the order of sharps is F. The second sharp is C. The distance from F to C is a fifth. The third sharp is G, which is a fifth above C, and so on.

              5th   5th

    F → C → G

3. Fill in the blanks to name the order of sharps. The fifth above any sharp is the next sharp in the order of sharps. The first one is done for you.

    The first sharp is _F_.   A fifth above _F_ is _C_.
    The second sharp is _C_.   A fifth above _C_ is ____.
    The third sharp is ____.   A fifth above ____ is ____.
    The fourth sharp is ____.   A fifth above ____ is ____.
    The fifth sharp is ____.   A fifth above ____ is ____.
    The sixth sharp is ____.   A fifth above ____ is ____.
    The seventh sharp is ____.

KEYS WITH FLATS

The left side of the circle contains keys with flats. As the circle moves clockwise in fifths, it moves counterclockwise in fourths.

As C Major is at the top of the circle, the next key to the left is the key that is an interval of a fourth above C, which is F Major.

The keys move around the circle counterclockwise in order of fourths, adding flats along the way so that the first flat key (F Major) has 1 flat, the next key (B♭ Major) has 2 flats, and so on.

$$C \xrightarrow{4th} F \xrightarrow{4th} B\flat$$

4. Fill in the blanks to name the Major keys that have flats as they move around the circle in order of fourths beginning with C Major. The fourth of one key is the next key in the circle. Remember that most of the flat keys have a flat in the key name (for example, A♭ Major). The first one is done for you.

No flats:	key of _C_ Major	A fourth above _C_ is _F_.
1 flat:	key of _F_ Major	A fourth above _F_ is ___.
2 flats:	key of ___ Major	A fourth above ___ is ___.
3 flats:	key of ___ Major	A fourth above ___ is ___.
4 flats:	key of ___ Major	A fourth above ___ is ___.
5 flats:	key of ___ Major	A fourth above ___ is ___.
6 flats:	key of ___ Major	A fourth above ___ is ___.
7 flats:	key of ___ Major	

The minor keys with flats also move in fourths.
Example: a minor to d minor is a fourth, d minor to g minor is a fourth, and so on.

$$a \xrightarrow{4th} d \xrightarrow{4th} g$$

5. Fill in the blanks to name the minor keys that have flats as they move around the circle in order of fourths beginning with a minor. The fourth of one key is the next key in the circle. The first one is done for you.

No flats: key of _a_ minor   A fourth above _a_ is _d_.
1 flat: key of _d_ minor   A fourth above _d_ is ___.
2 flats: key of ___ minor   A fourth above ___ is ___.
3 flats: key of ___ minor   A fourth above ___ is ___.
4 flats: key of ___ minor   A fourth above ___ is ___.
5 flats: key of ___ minor   A fourth above ___ is ___.
6 flats: key of ___ minor   A fourth above ___ is ___.
7 flats: key of ___ minor

THE ORDER OF FLATS

Just as the order of keys with flats moves in fourths, the order of flats also moves in fourths!

Example: The first flat in the order of flats is B. The second flat is E. The distance from B to E is a fourth. The third flat is A, which is a fourth above E, and so on.

                   4th   4th

         B   →   E   →   A

6. Fill in the blanks to name the order of flats. The fourth above any flat is the next flat in the order of flats. The first one is done for you.

     The first flat is _B_. A fourth above _B_ is _E_.

     The second flat is _E_. A fourth above _E_ is ___.

     The third flat is ___. A fourth above ___ is ___.

     The fourth flat is ___. A fourth above ___ is ___.

     The fifth flat is ___. A fourth above ___ is ___.

     The sixth flat is ___. A fourth above ___ is ___.

     The seventh flat is ___.

7. Complete the circle of fifths below by adding:
    Major keys
    Minor keys
    Key signatures

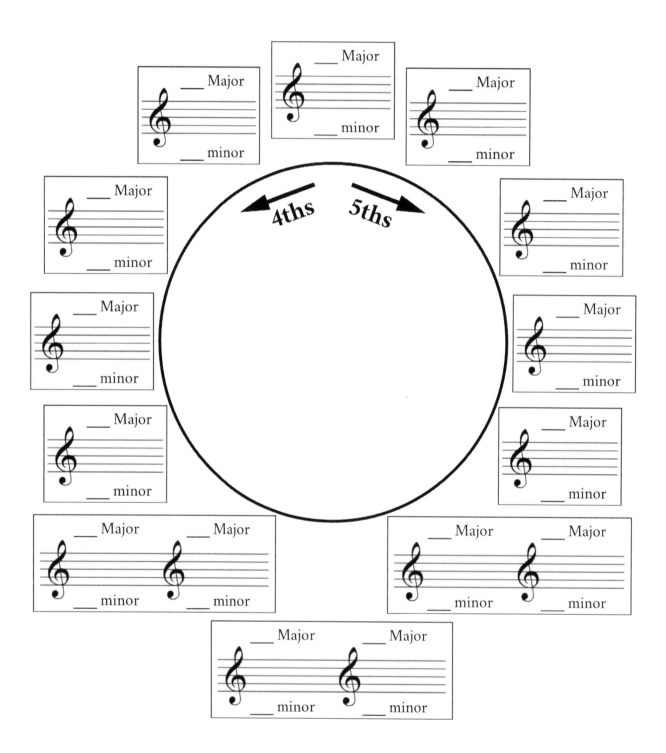

CHAPTER 8

Triads

Triads are the building blocks of chords. Triads have three notes. Each note is an interval of a 3rd above the note below it. The bottom note, which we call the root note, is the name of the triad.

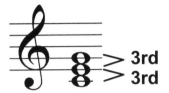

Example: The root note of this triad is C. The middle note, E, is an interval of a 3rd above the C. The top note, G, is a 3rd above the E.

MAJOR TRIADS

When the upper two notes of the triad belong to the Major key of the root note (bottom note) of the triad, it is a **Major triad**.

Examples:

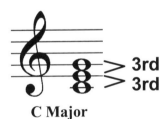

C Major

This is a C Major triad. As the key of C Major has no sharps or flats, all of the notes in the C Major triad are natural (not sharp or flat).

D Major

This is a D Major triad. As the F is sharp in the key of D Major, the F is sharp in the D Major triad.

1. Draw the **upper two notes** above each given root note to complete the **Major triads** and write the name of the triad on the line under the staff. Include sharp or flat signs when needed. Major triads are named with UPPERCASE letters. The first one is done for you.

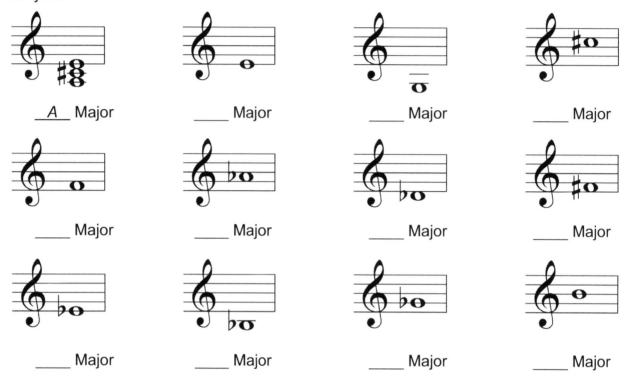

MINOR TRIADS

When the middle note of a Major triad is lowered a half step, the triad becomes minor.

Examples:

A Major   a minor

As the middle note of the A Major triad is C sharp, the middle note of the a minor triad is C natural, which is a half step below C sharp.

52

G Major g minor

As the middle note of the G Major triad is B natural, the middle note of the g minor triad is B flat, which is a half step below B natural.

2. Draw the **upper two notes** above each root note to complete the **minor triads** and write the name of the triad on the line under the staff. Include sharp or flat signs when needed. Minor triads are named with lowercase letters. The first one is done for you.

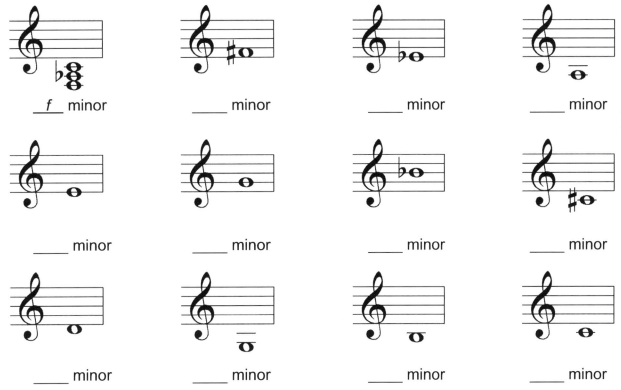

3. Check whether each triad is Major or minor. The first one is done for you.

____ Major
  X minor

____ Major
____ minor

____ Major
____ minor

____ Major
____ minor

____ Major
____ minor

____ Major
____ minor

____ Major
____ minor

____ Major
____ minor

____ Major
____ minor

____ Major
____ minor

____ Major
____ minor

____ Major
____ minor

____ Major
____ minor

____ Major
____ minor

____ Major
____ minor

____ Major
____ minor

CHAPTER 9

Chords

Triads can also be called **chords**. The notes of a chord can appear in any order and the root note does not have to be the lowest note.

Here are two examples of chords:

To find the names of these chords, first name each note within the chords.

   Notes:
F#
D
A

   Notes:
C
A
E

Next, put the note names in order of 3rds so that they form a triad.

   Notes: Triad:
F#   A
D   F#
A   D

   Notes: Triad:
C   E
A   C
E   A

55

Then, name the chords based on the root notes, which are the lowest notes of each triad, and name whether they are Major or minor.

Notes: Triad: Chord name:
F#   A   **D Major**
D   F#
A   D

Notes: Triad: Chord name:
C   E   **a minor**
A   C
E   A

1. Name the chords. First, write the note names in any order, then write the notes in order of a triad with the root note on the bottom and name the chord. Major chords are named with UPPERCASE letters and minor chords are named with lowercase letters. For example, E Major or e minor. The first one is done for you.

Notes: Triad: Chord name:
_F#_   _F#_   _b minor_
_B_   _D_
_D_   _B_

Notes: Triad: Chord name:
____   ____   _____
____   ____
____   ____

Notes: Triad: Chord name:
____   ____   _____
____   ____
____   ____

Notes: Triad: Chord name:
____   ____   _____
____   ____
____   ____

56

	Notes:	Triad:	Chord name:
(staff: C-E-G)	___ ___ ___	___ ___ ___	_____

	Notes:	Triad:	Chord name:
(staff: D-F#-A)	___ ___ ___	___ ___ ___	_____

	Notes:	Triad:	Chord name:
(staff: E-G#-B#)	___ ___ ___	___ ___ ___	_____

	Notes:	Triad:	Chord name:
(staff: Bb-D-F)	___ ___ ___	___ ___ ___	_____

	Notes:	Triad:	Chord name:
(staff: G-Bb-D)	___ ___ ___	___ ___ ___	_____

	Notes:	Triad:	Chord name:
(staff: C-Eb-G)	___ ___ ___	___ ___ ___	_____

	Notes:	Triad:	Chord name:
(staff: A-C#-E)	___ ___ ___	___ ___ ___	_____

Chords can have more than three notes. They can have any combination of the three notes in the triad. Some notes may be doubled or tripled.

Examples:

Notes:	Triad:	Chord name:
F♯	A	D Major
D	F♯	
D	D	
A		

Notes:	Triad:	Chord name:
G	D	G Major
B	B	
G	G	
D		
B		

2. Fill in the blanks to determine the name of each chord.

Notes: Triad: Chord name:
_____   _____   _____
_____   _____
_____
_____
_____

Notes: Triad: Chord name:
_____   _____   _____
_____   _____
_____
_____
_____

Notes: Triad: Chord name:
_____   _____   _____
_____   _____
_____
_____
_____

	Notes:	Triad:	Chord name:
(staff 1)	___	___	_____
	___	___	
	___	___	
	___		

	Notes:	Triad:	Chord name:
(staff 2)	___	___	_____
	___	___	
	___	___	
	___		

	Notes:	Triad:	Chord name:
(staff 3)	___	___	_____
	___	___	
	___	___	
	___		
	___		
	___		

	Notes:	Triad:	Chord name:
(staff 4)	___	___	_____
	___	___	
	___	___	
	___		

	Notes:	Triad:	Chord name:
(staff 5)	___	___	_____
	___	___	
	___	___	
	___		

	Notes:	Triad:	Chord name:
(staff 6)	___	___	_____
	___	___	
	___	___	
	___		

3. Name the chords using the fretboard charts. They can be Major chords or minor chords. The first one is done for you.

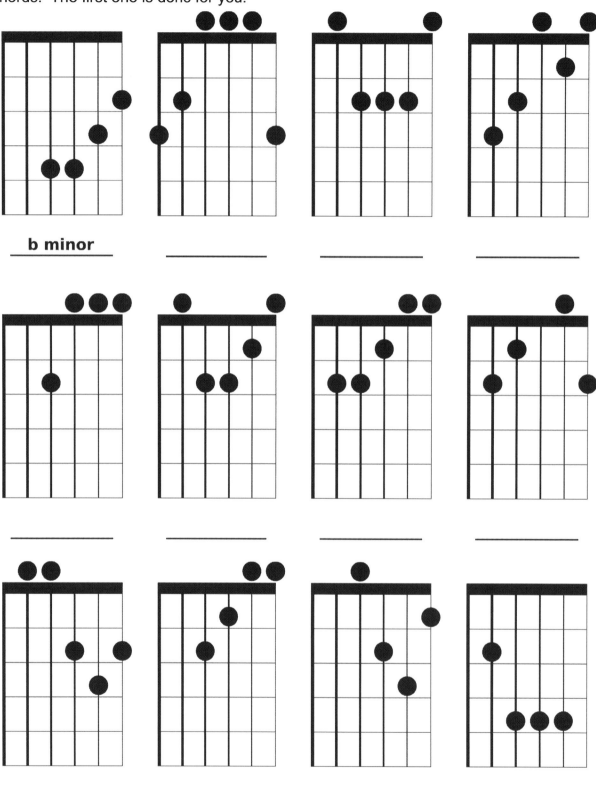

b minor

DOMINANT 7 CHORDS

Dominant 7 chords are built on the Dominant (5th scale degree). They contain the **Major triad** with an **added minor 7th note**.

Example:

The C Dominant 7 chord contains the C Major triad (C, E, and G) + the minor 7th (B♭).

C Dominant 7

Dominant 7 chords can contain any combination of notes that belong to the chord.

Example:

Dominant 7 chords can also be labeled as Dom 7 or simply 7. For example, a G Dominant 7 can also be called G Dom7 or G7.

G7

4. Name the Dominant 7 chords below. Label them as A7, G7, etc. The first one is done for you.

   A7   _____   _____   _____

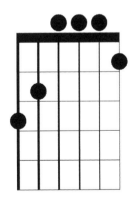 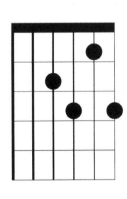 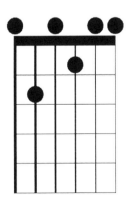 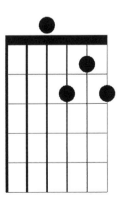

ARPEGGIOS

Chords can also be played as **arpeggios**, in which the notes of a chord are played separately.

Examples:

The notes in this arpeggio - G, B, and D, make up a G Major chord.

The notes of this arpeggio - E, G♯, B, and D, make up an E7 chord.

5. Name the chords below each arpeggio.

CHAPTER 10

Barre Chords

In a barre chord, the first finger lies straight across a fret, fretting more than one string. All of the notes in a barre chord are fretted, so barre chord shapes are moveable!

ROOT SIX BARRE CHORDS

Root six barre chords have root notes on the sixth string. Let's review the names of the notes across the sixth string. Here are all the sixth string notes:

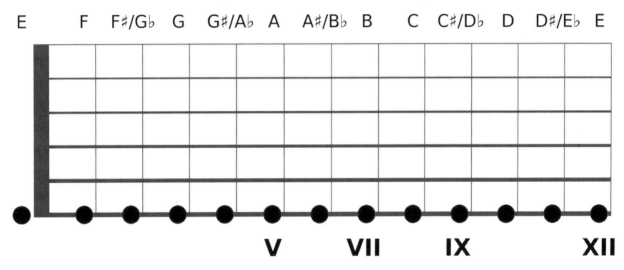

1. Name the 6th string notes below.

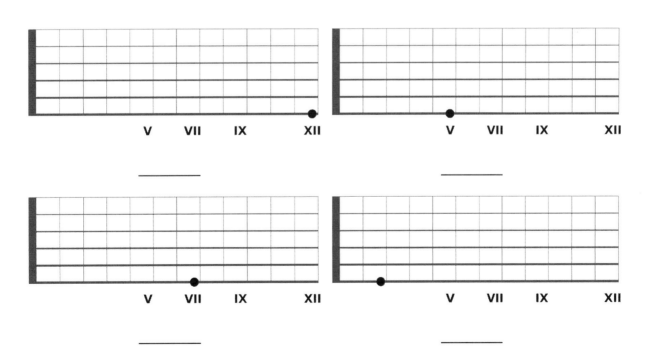

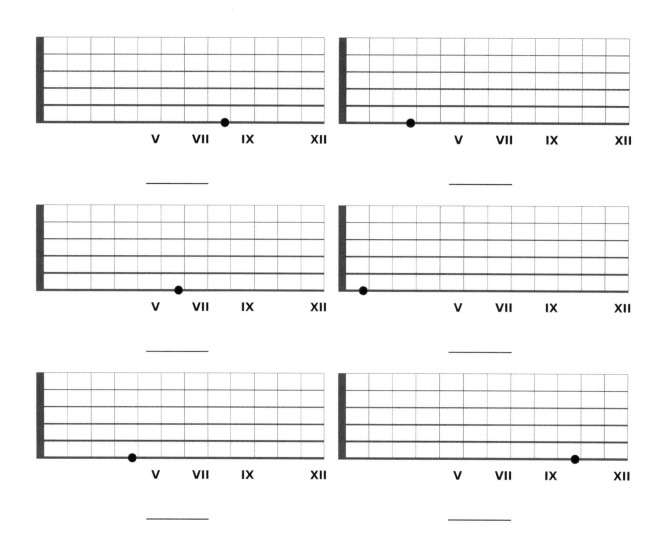

Root six barre chords are based on the **E chord shapes** as E is the open sixth string.

Root six Major chords:

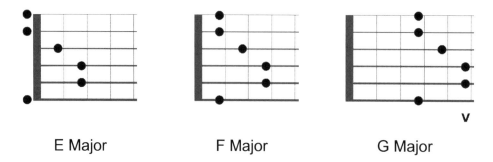

E Major   F Major   G Major

Notice that the Major chords are all based on the E shape. The F Major has F as its root note on the sixth string and the G Major has G as its root note on the sixth string.

Root six minor chords:

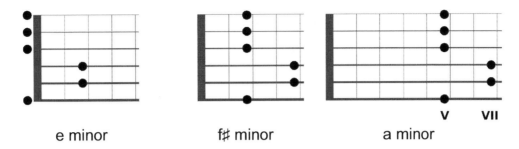

Notice that the minor chords are all based on the e minor shape. The root notes which name the chords are all on the sixth string.

Root six Dominant 7 chords:

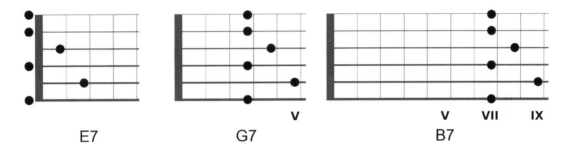

The Dominant 7 chords are all based on the E7 shape and the root notes are all on the sixth string.

2. Name the root six barre chords below. The first one is done for you.

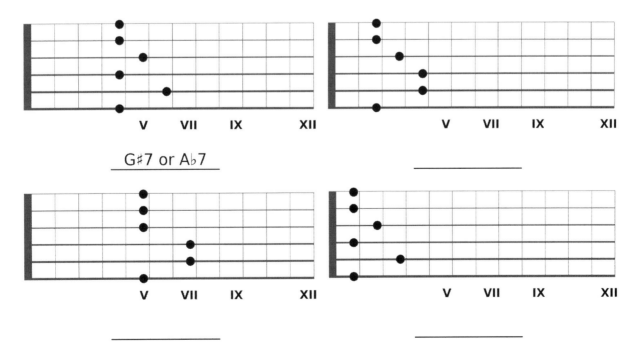

G♯7 or A♭7

65

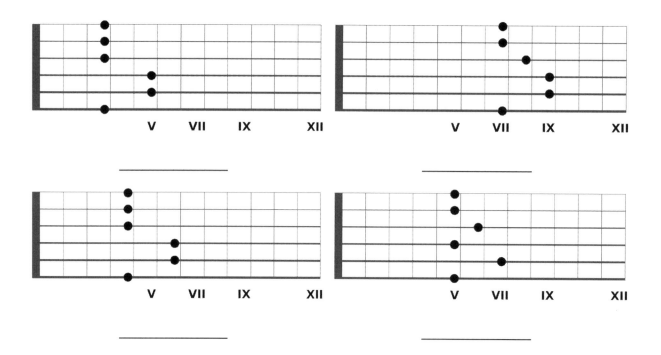

ROOT FIVE BARRE CHORDS

Root five barre chords have root notes on the fifth string. Let's review the names of the notes across the fifth string. Here are all the fifth string notes:

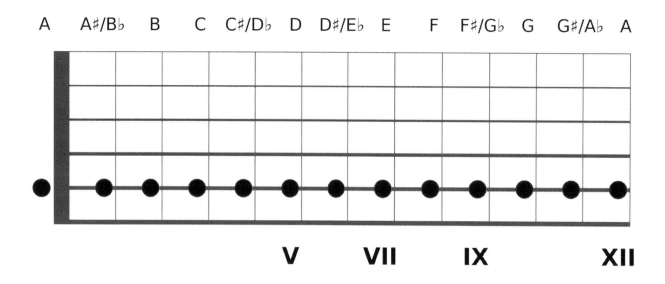

3. Name the fifth string notes below.

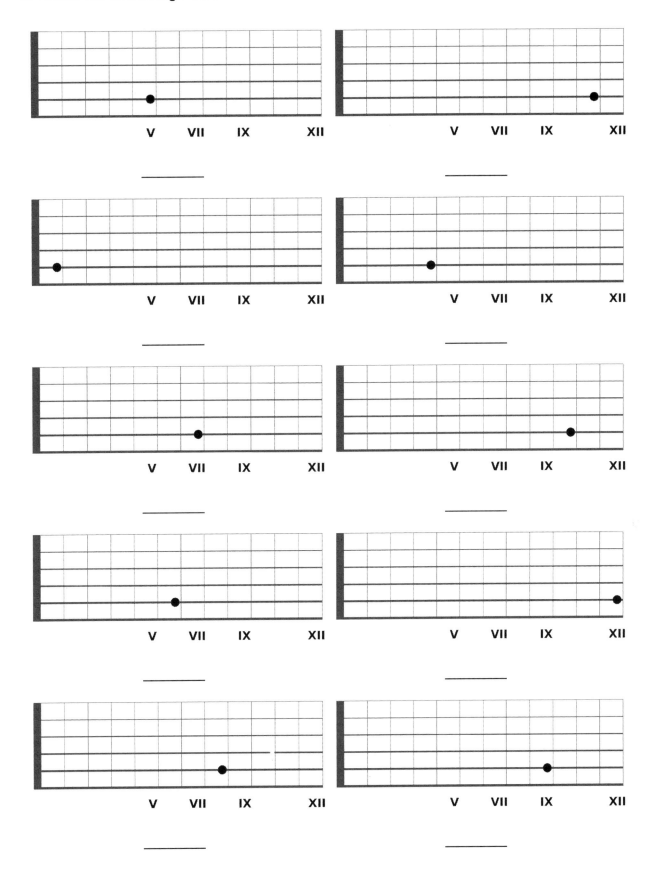

Root five barre chords are based on the **A chord shapes** as A is the open fifth string.

Root five Major chords:

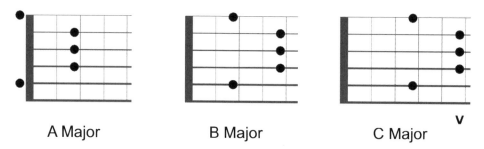

A Major   B Major   C Major

Notice that the Major chords are all based on the A shape. The B Major has B as its root note on the fifth string and the C Major has C as its root note on the fifth string.

Root five minor chords:

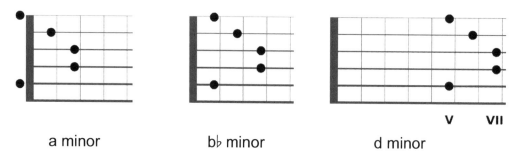

a minor   b♭ minor   d minor

Notice that the minor chords are all based on the a minor shape. The root notes which name the chords are all on the fifth string.

Root five Dominant 7 chords:

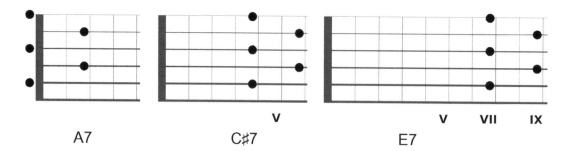

A7   C♯7   E7

The Dominant 7 chords are all based on the A7 shape and the root notes are all on the fifth string.

4. Name the root five barre chords below. The first one is done for you.

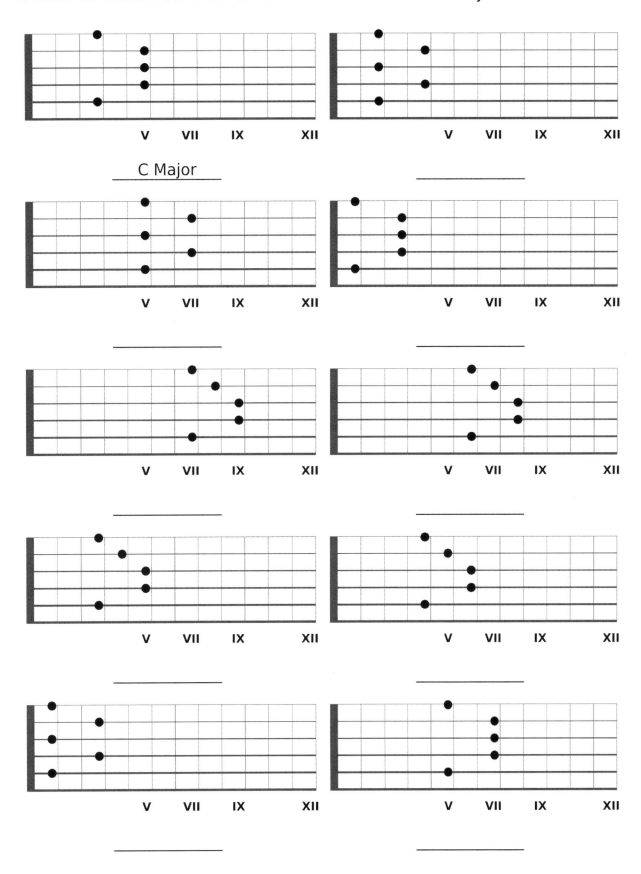

Putting it all together - Root five and root six barre chords combined.

5. Name the barre chords below.

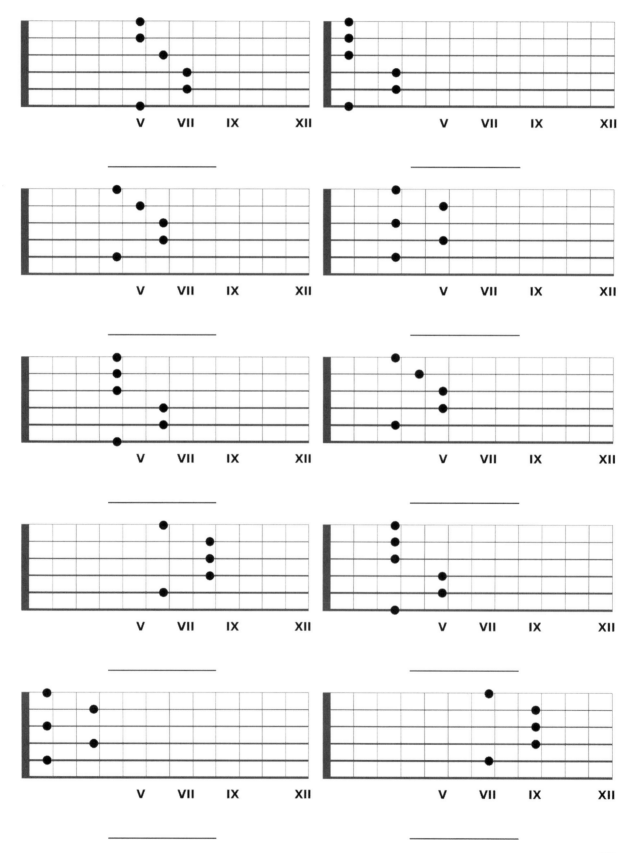

CHAPTER 11

Cadences

A **cadence** is a chord progression at the end of a song or musical phrase. Roman numerals are used to represent scale degrees within each chord. For example, in the key of C Major the I chord is C, the IV chord is F (the fourth note of the C Major scale), and the V chord is G (the fifth note of the C Major scale).

Here are three types of cadences. Notice that the cadence examples contain key signatures, so there is no need for sharp or flat signs next to the notes.

Authentic Cadence:

V - I

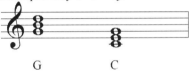

or

V⁷ - I

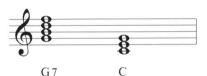

Plagal Cadence:

IV - I

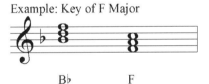

Half Cadence:

I - V

or

I - V⁷

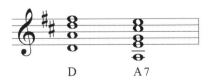

1. Label the chords with Roman numerals and check the correct cadence. Use the key signature to determine the Major key. The first example is done for you.

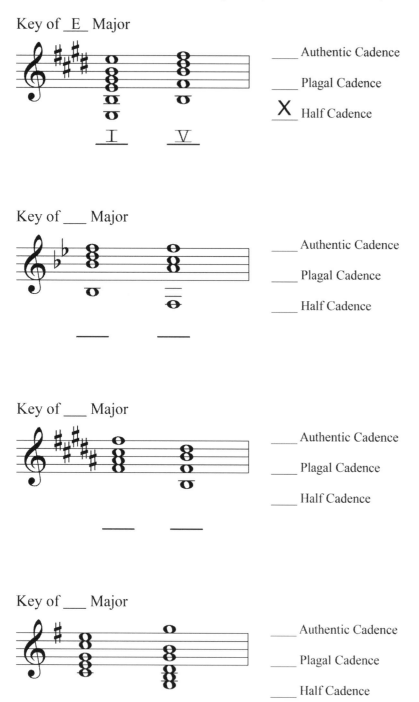

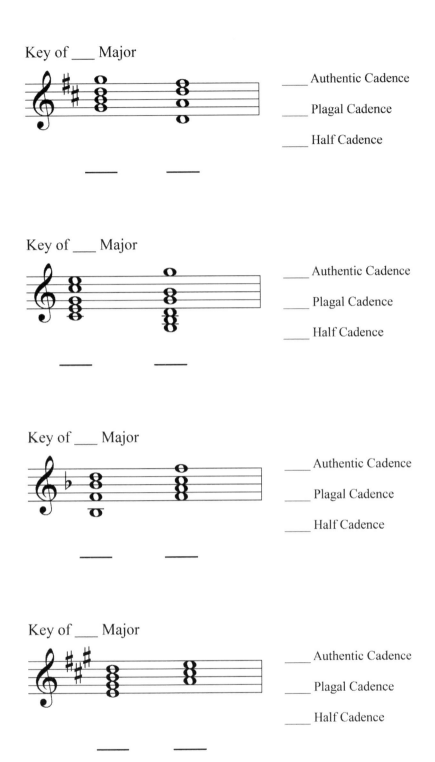

73

2. Draw chords to create each cadence and write the Roman numerals under each chord. Follow the key signatures. You can draw 3, 4, 5, or 6-note chords with the notes in any order. Authentic and half cadences can include the V or V⁷ chord. The first one is done for you.

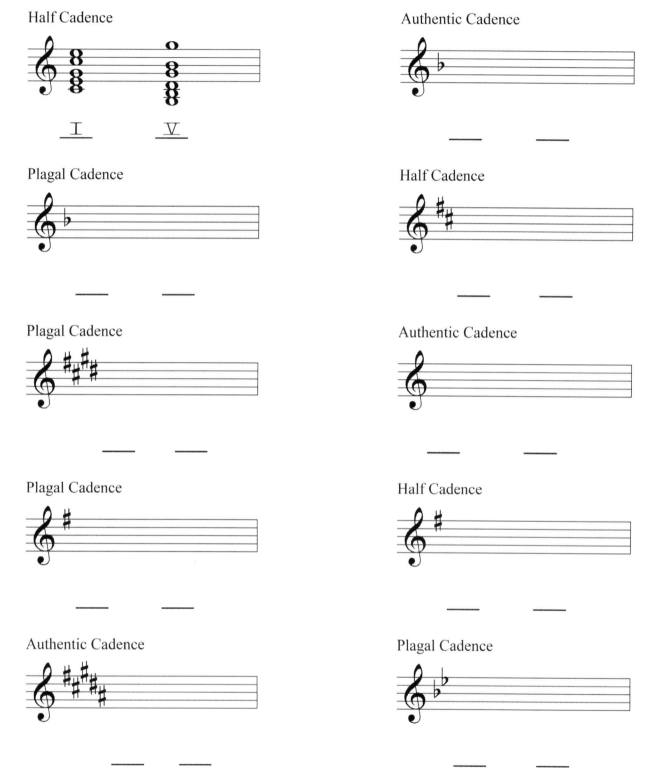

Authentic Cadence   Half Cadence

   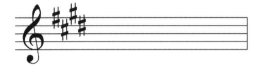

          ___   ___   ___   ___

Plagal Cadence   Plagal Cadence

   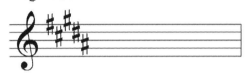

          ___   ___   ___   ___

3. Check the type of cadence that ends each music example and label the last two chords which create the cadence with Roman numerals.

___ Authentic Cadence   ___ Plagal Cadence   ___ Half Cadence

___ Authentic Cadence   ___ Plagal Cadence   ___ Half Cadence   ___   ___

___ Authentic Cadence   ___ Plagal Cadence   ___ Half Cadence   ___   ___

CHAPTER 12

Chord Progressions

CHORD SCALES

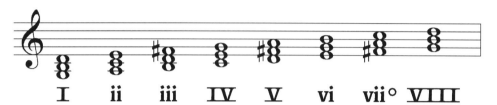

This is an example of a **chord scale** built on G Major.

The I, IV, and V (and VIII) chords of a chord scale are Major, the ii, iii, and vi chords are minor, and the vii° is diminished. These chord qualities are true for chord scales built on any Major scale as long as the notes within the key are maintained. For example, in the G chord scale above, all Fs are sharp as the G Major scale has an F sharp.

The V chord can also be written as V7.
Example:

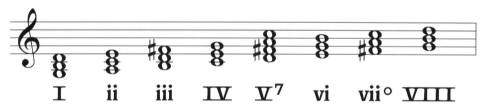

Another way to write a chord scale is to include a key signature at the beginning so that the sharps and flats don't need to be written into each chord.
Example:

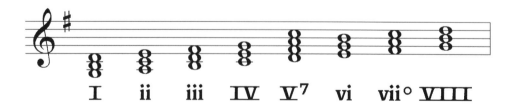

76

1. Write chord scales for the following Major keys. Draw triads. Draw sharp or flat signs next to the notes when needed (do **not** include key signatures). Write the Roman numerals under each chord. As in the previous examples, Roman numerals should be UPPERCASE for Major chords and lowercase for minor or diminished chords. You can choose to write either a V or V⁷ for the fifth scale degree. The first one is done for you.

D Major

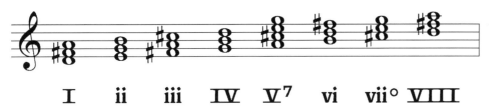

A Major

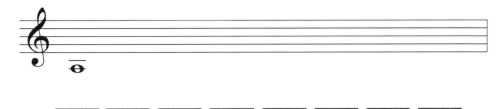

E Major

B Major

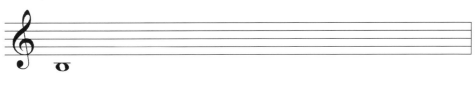

F Major

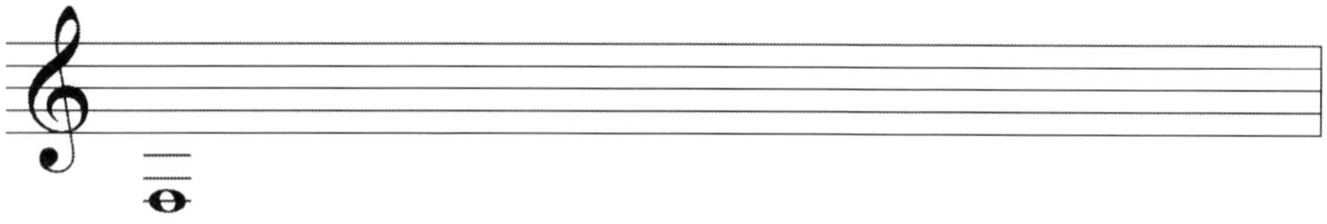

___ ___ ___ ___ ___ ___ ___ ___

B♭ Major

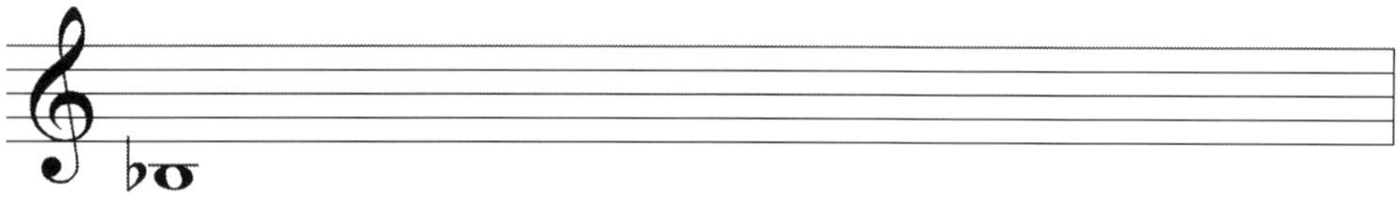

___ ___ ___ ___ ___ ___ ___ ___

2. Complete the chart below by adding chord names for all given keys. Begin by writing in the names of the notes in each scale and then add the chord qualities (lowercase m for minor or ° for diminished). Some are done for you.

Key	I	ii	iii	IV	V	vi	vii°
C Major							
G Major							
D Major							
A Major							
E Major							
B Major							
F♯ Major	F♯	g♯m	a♯m	B	C♯	d♯m	e♯°
F Major							
B♭ Major							
E♭ Major							
A♭ Major							
D♭ Major							
G♭ Major	G♭	a♭m	b♭m	C♭	D♭	e♭m	f°

CHORD PROGRESSIONS

A chord progression is a series of chords.

An example of a chord progression is:

    I - IV - V - I

Let's look at this chord progression in two different keys.

Key of C Major:				Key of B♭ Major:			
C	F	G	C	B♭	E♭	F	B♭
I	IV	V	I	I	IV	V	I

3. Write the chord progressions for each given key. The first one is done for you.

Chord Progression:	I	-	ii	-	V^7	-	I
Key of G Major:	G		am		D7		G
Key of D Major:	___		___		___		___
Key of A Major:	___		___		___		___
Key of E Major:	___		___		___		___
Key of B Major:	___		___		___		___
Key of F Major:	___		___		___		___
Key of B♭ Major:	___		___		___		___
Key of E♭ Major:	___		___		___		___

Chord Progression:	I	-	iii	-	vi	-	ii	-	V	-	I
Key of G Major:	___		___		___		___		___		___
Key of D Major:	___		___		___		___		___		___
Key of A Major:	___		___		___		___		___		___
Key of E Major:	___		___		___		___		___		___
Key of B Major:	___		___		___		___		___		___
Key of F Major:	___		___		___		___		___		___
Key of B♭ Major:	___		___		___		___		___		___
Key of E♭ Major:	___		___		___		___		___		___

Chord Progression:	vi	-	IV	-	I	-	V^7
Key of G Major:	___		___		___		___
Key of D Major:	___		___		___		___
Key of A Major:	___		___		___		___
Key of E Major:	___		___		___		___
Key of B Major:	___		___		___		___
Key of F Major:	___		___		___		___
Key of B♭ Major:	___		___		___		___
Key of E♭ Major:	___		___		___		___

4. Write the Roman numerals and names of the chords for each chord progression. There are no sharp or flat signs next to the notes as the key signatures are given. The first example is done for you.

Key of F Major:

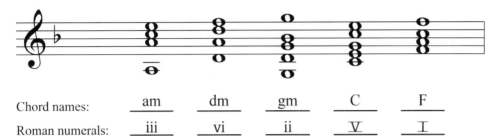

Chord names: am   dm   gm   C   F
Roman numerals: iii   vi   ii   V   I

Key of C Major:

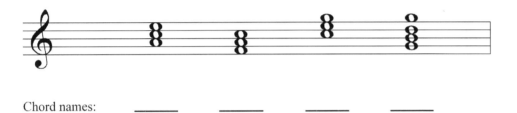

Chord names: _____ _____ _____ _____
Roman numerals: _____ _____ _____ _____

Key of G Major:

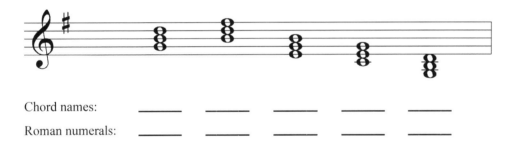

Chord names: _____ _____ _____ _____ _____
Roman numerals: _____ _____ _____ _____ _____

Key of D Major:

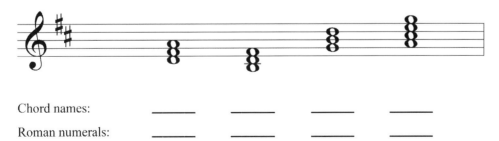

Chord names: _____ _____ _____ _____
Roman numerals: _____ _____ _____ _____

Key of A Major:

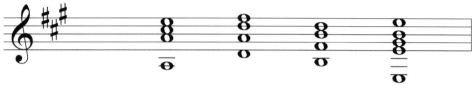

Chord names:

Roman numerals:

Key of E Major:

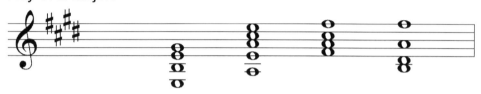

Chord names:

Roman numerals:

Key of F Major:

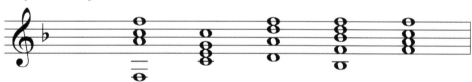

Chord names:

Roman numerals:

Key of B♭ Major:

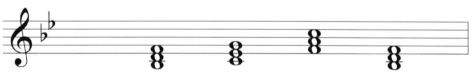

Chord names:

Roman numerals:

5. Label the arpeggios with Roman numerals and chord names. The first example is done for you.

Key of C Major:

Chord names: C   F   G   C
Roman numerals: I   IV   V   I

Key of D Major:

Chord names: _____   _____   _____   _____
Roman numerals: _____   _____   _____   _____

Key of A Major:

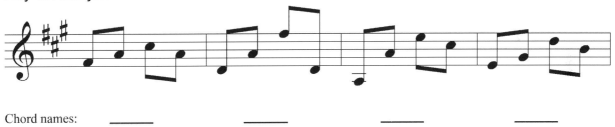

Chord names: _____   _____   _____   _____
Roman numerals: _____   _____   _____   _____

Key of E Major:

Chord names: _____   _____   _____   _____
Roman numerals: _____   _____   _____   _____

6. Write your own chord progression, then play it to hear how it sounds!

Key of _____ Major

Chord names:

Roman numerals:

CHAPTER 13

Transposition

To **transpose** music means to put it in a different key.

TRANSPOSING CHORD PROGRESSIONS

We can transpose any chord progression by determining the scale degrees with Roman numerals and chord qualities (Major, minor, Dominant 7, etc.) and placing those same scale degrees and chord qualities in a different key.

Example:

Here is a chord progression in the key of C Major:

C	G	am	F	C
I	V	vi	IV	I

When we place the chords with the same Roman numerals in the key of D Major, keeping Major chords Major and minor chords minor, we get the following chord progression:

D	A	bm	G	D
I	V	vi	IV	I

1. Write the Roman numerals for each chord progression and transpose them to the given keys. The first one is done for you.

Key of A Major:	A	D	E7	A
	I	IV	V^7	I

Transpose to the key of E Major:	E	A	B7	E
	I	IV	V^7	I

Key of D Major: D   A   bm   G   D
                     ___   ___   ___   ___   ___

Transpose to the   ___   ___   ___   ___   ___
key of B Major:

Key of F Major: F   C   dm   B♭   F
                     ___   ___   ___   ___   ___

Transpose to the   ___   ___   ___   ___   ___
key of B♭ Major:

Key of G Major: G   bm   C   D7   G
                     ___   ___   ___   ___   ___

Transpose to the   ___   ___   ___   ___   ___
key of A Major:

Key of E Major: c♯m   f♯m   B7   E
                     ___   ___   ___   ___

Transpose to the   ___   ___   ___   ___
key of C Major:

TRANSPOSING MELODIES

Here is an example of the same melody written in two different keys.

"Jingle Bells"

Key of C Major:

Key of D Major:

Play both melodies. Notice that they are the same melody, but that the melody in the key of D Major sounds higher.

Here are the steps to transpose a melody:

1. **Determine the starting note.**

To find the starting note, determine the scale degree that the song starts on. In the key of C Major, *Jingle Bells* begins on the 3rd note of the C Major key, which is E, so the starting note for transposing it to the key of D will be the third note of the D Major key, which is F♯.

2. **Determine the distance between the original key and key you're transposing to.**

In the example above, the original key is C and we are transposing to D. The distance from C to D is up a Major 2nd.

3. **Transpose all the notes according to the distance between the two keys.**

Notice that all of the notes in *Jingle Bells* are a Major 2nd higher in the key of D than they are in the key of C. If you maintain the key signature, you will not have to add any additional sharps or flats when transposing.

Here is another example of a melody in two different keys.

"Amazing Grace"

Key of G Major:

Key of D Major:

In this example, rather than transposing up a fifth from G to D, it is transposed down a fourth from G to D. Sometimes it works better to transpose down rather than up. You can look at the lowest and the highest note of the song to determine which is a better method for the song you're transposing.

Notice that all of the notes in *Amazing Grace* are an interval of a fourth lower in the key of D than they are in the key of G.

2. Transpose the **melody** for *"Ode to Joy"* from the original key of F Major to the keys of C Major and G Major. Transpose **up** rather than down for both keys. Then transpose the **chord progression** by writing the chords above the music as seen in the original key of F. Play the song in each key to check your work!

Key of F Major:

Key of C Major:

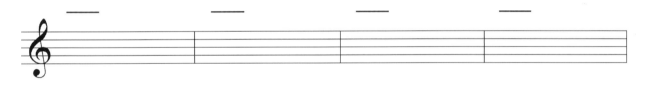

Key of G Major:

3. Transpose the **melody** and **chord progression** for *"Aura Lee"* from the original key of C Major to the keys of F Major and G Major. Transpose **down** rather than up for both keys. Play the song in each key to check your work!

Key of C Major:

Key of F Major:

Key of G Major:

CHAPTER 14

Rhythms

NOTE VALUES in 4/4 time

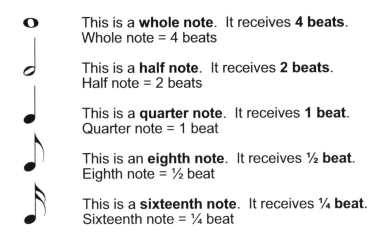

1. How many beats does each note receive in 4/4 time?

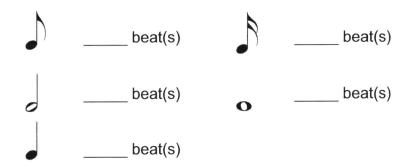

When two eighth notes are next to each other, they are connected with a line at the top called a **beam**. As each eighth note by itself receives ½ beat, two eighth notes together receive 1 beat.

When sixteenth notes are next to each other, they are also connected with a beam. As each sixteenth note receives ¼ beat, four sixteenth notes together equal one whole beat.

1/4 beat + 1/4 beat + 1/4 beat + 1/4 beat = 1 beat

Eighth notes and sixteenth notes can also be connected in the combinations below. When added together, each group receives one beat.

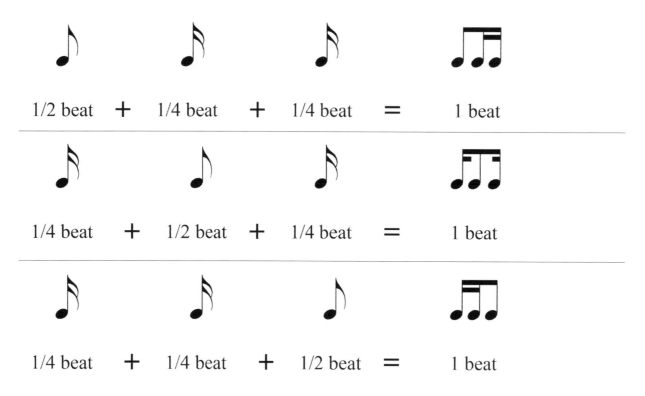

1/2 beat + 1/4 beat + 1/4 beat = 1 beat

1/4 beat + 1/2 beat + 1/4 beat = 1 beat

1/4 beat + 1/4 beat + 1/2 beat = 1 beat

Four eighth notes can also be connected. As each eighth note receives ½ beat, four eighth notes together receive 2 beats.

1/2 beat + 1/2 beat + 1/2 beat + 1/2 beat = 2 beats

TRIPLETS

Each eighth note **triplet** receives ⅓ **beat**, so combined together, all three triplets equal one beat.

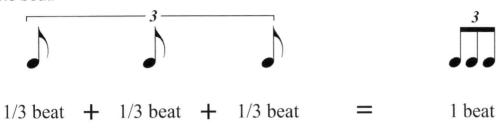

1/3 beat   +   1/3 beat   +   1/3 beat   =   1 beat

2. Write the number of beats each note receives. The first one is done for you.

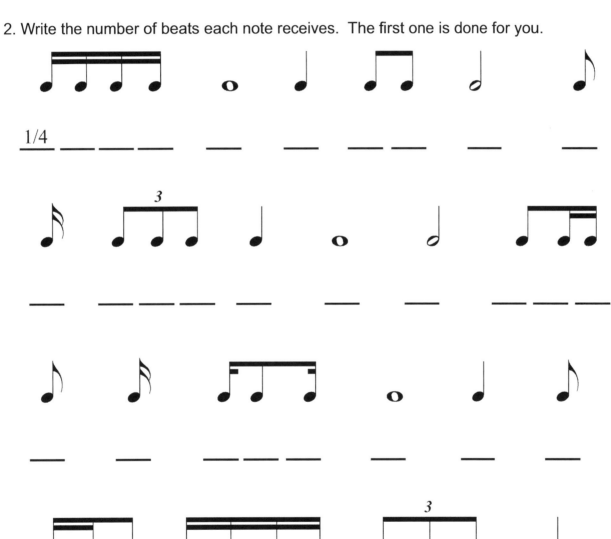

3. How many beats does each group of notes receive when added together? The first one is done for you.

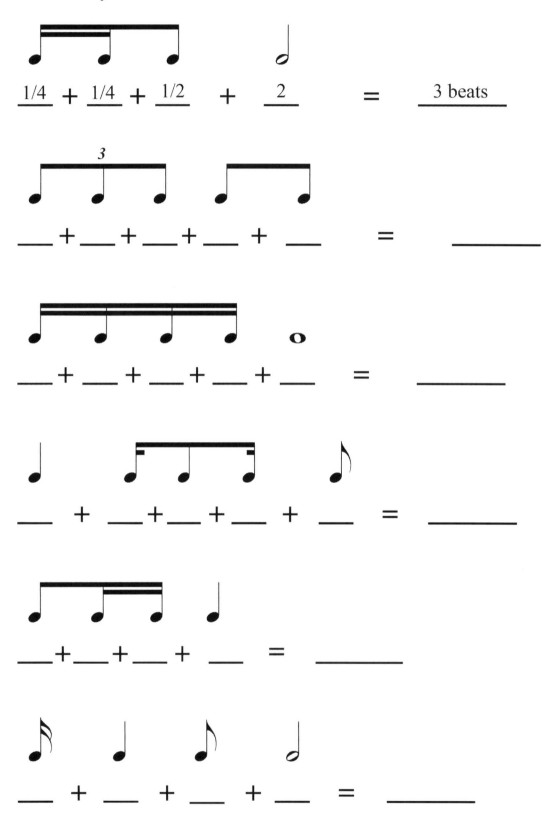

CHAPTER 15

Dotted Rhythms

When a dot is placed after a note, it adds half of the note value to the note.

 This is a **dotted half note**. As a half note receives 2 beats, the dotted half note receives **3 beats**.
Dotted half note = 3 beats

 This is a **dotted quarter note**. As a quarter note receives 1 beat, the dotted quarter note receives **1 ½ beats**.
Dotted quarter note = 1 ½ beats

 This is a **dotted eighth note**. As an eighth note receives ½ beat, the dotted eighth note receives **¾ beat** (½ + ¼).
Dotted eighth note = ¾ beat

Dotted eighth notes can be beamed with sixteenth notes.

1. How many beats do these notes receive?

2. How many beats do these groups of notes receive when added together? The first one is done for you.

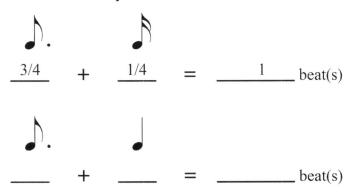

95

𝅗𝅥.   𝅘𝅥.

____ + ____ = _____ beat(s)

♪.   ♪.

____ + ____ = _____ beat(s)

𝅗𝅥   𝅘𝅥

____ + ____ = _____ beat(s)

𝅗𝅥.   o

____ + ____ = _____ beat(s)

𝅘𝅥.   𝅗𝅥.

____ + ____ = _____ beat(s)

𝅗𝅥.   ♪

____ + ____ = _____ beat(s)

3. Draw one note in each box so that each group of notes equals 4 beats. The first one is done for you.

𝅘𝅥. + ♪ + ♪ + [𝅘𝅥.]   =   4 beats

𝅘𝅥 + 𝅗𝅥 + ♪ + [   ]   =   4 beats

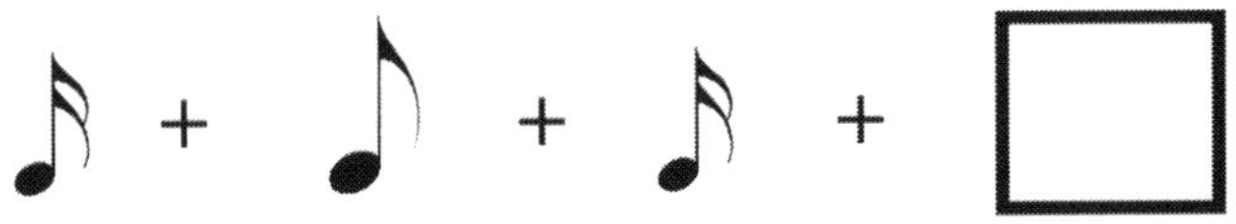

♫ + ♪ + ♪ + ☐ = 4 beats

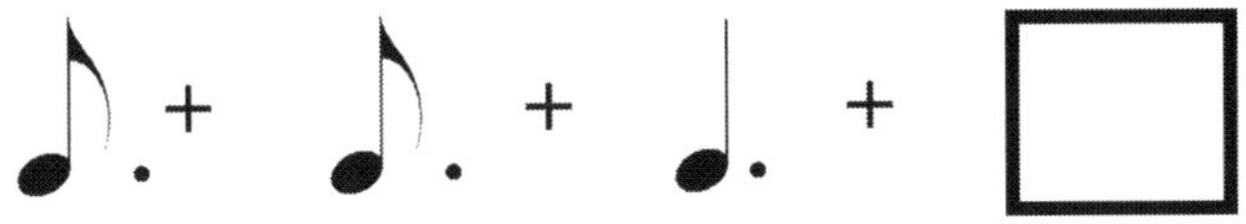

♪. + ♪. + ♩. + ☐ = 4 beats

4. Draw one note in each box to complete each question below. The first one is done for you.

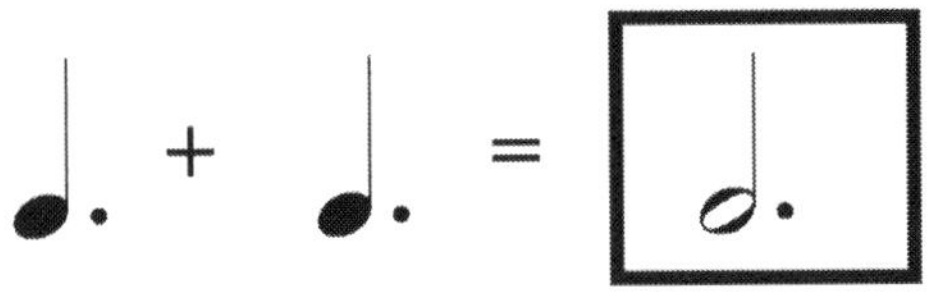

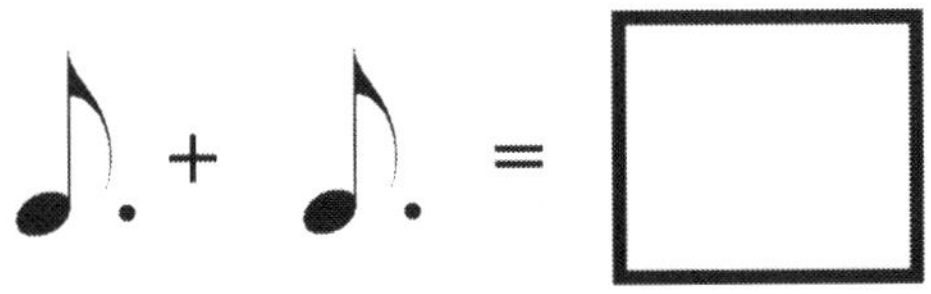

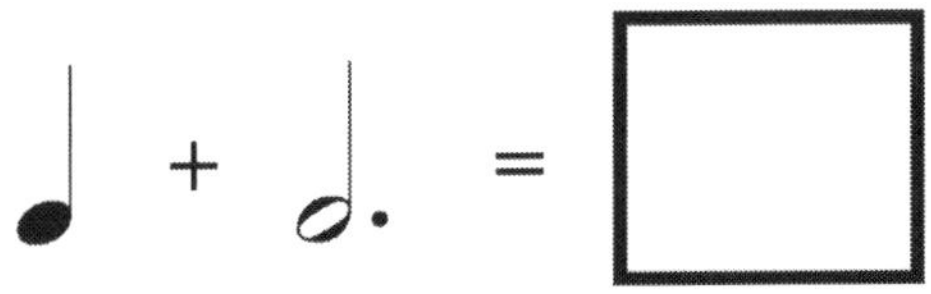

♩. + ♩. = ☐ 𝅗𝅥.

♪. + ♪. = ☐

♩ + ♩. = ☐

♪. + ♫ = ☐

♫ + ♫ + ♫ = ☐

♪. + ♪. + ♪ = ☐

CHAPTER 16

Rests

Here are some different rests that are used in music. When in 4/4 time, as a whole note receives 4 beats, the whole rest also receives 4 beats. As the dotted half note receives 3 beats, the dotted half rest also receives 3 beats, and so on.
*The whole rest can also mean to rest for the entire measure within any time signature.

Name	Symbol	Number of beats
Whole rest		4, or the entire measure
Dotted half rest		3
Half rest		2
Dotted quarter rest		1 1/2
Quarter rest		1
Dotted eighth rest		3/4
Eighth rest		1/2
Sixteenth rest		1/4

1. How many beats do these rests receive?

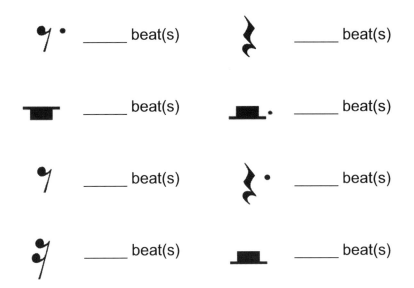

2. Draw a line connecting the rest in the left column to the note in the right column that has the same number of beats. The first one is done for you.

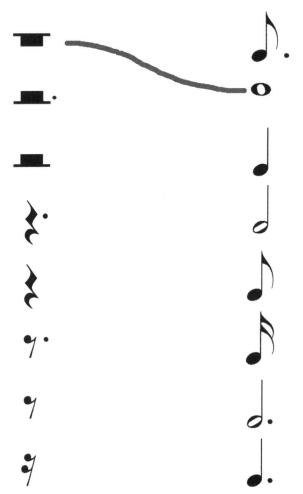

3. Write the number of beats each note or rest receives under the notes and rests. The first one is done for you.

4. How many beats do these notes and rests receive when added together? The first one is done for you.

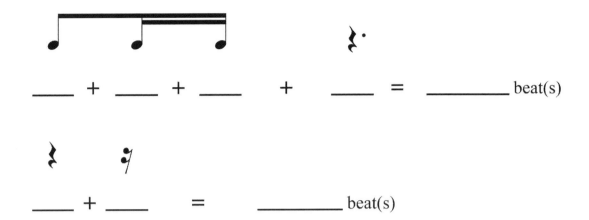

___ + ___ + ___ + ___ = _____ beat(s)

___ + ___ = _____ beat(s)

5. Draw one **rest** in each box so that each group of notes and rests equals 4 beats. The first one is done for you.

𝅗𝅥 + 𝄽· + ♪ + [𝄽] = 4 beats

𝄽· + ♪ + 𝄾 + [ ] = 4 beats

𝄾 + ♪. + 𝄽 + [ ] = 4 beats

♩ + 𝅗𝅥 + 𝄽· + [ ] = 4 beats

101

CHAPTER 17

Time Signatures

There are two numbers in a **time signature**. The top number tells us how many beats are in a measure. The bottom number tells us which note receives one beat.

When the bottom number of a time signature is 4, the quarter note receives one beat.

4/4 4 beats per measure
Quarter note = one beat

3/4 3 beats per measure
Quarter note = one beat

2/4 2 beats per measure
Quarter note = one beat

When the bottom number of a time signature is 2, the half note receives one beat.

2/2 2 beats per measure
Half note = one beat

When the bottom number of a time signature is 8, the eighth note receives one beat.

3/8 3 beats per measure
Eighth note = one beat

6/8 6 beats per measure
Eighth note = one beat

As 4/4 is the most common time signature, this is also called **common time** and is represented by the ¢ symbol.

4/4 = C

2/2 is also called **cut time** and is represented by the ¢ symbol.

2/2 = ¢

102

1. Fill in the blanks. The first one is done for you.

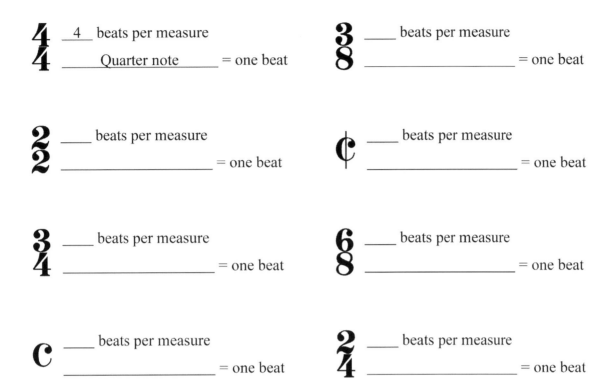

Here are examples of note values when the quarter note receives one beat. The equivalent rests receive the same number of beats as each note; for example, if a whole note receives 4 beats, the whole rest also receives 4 beats.

Note values in 2/4, 3/4, and 4/4, or c time:

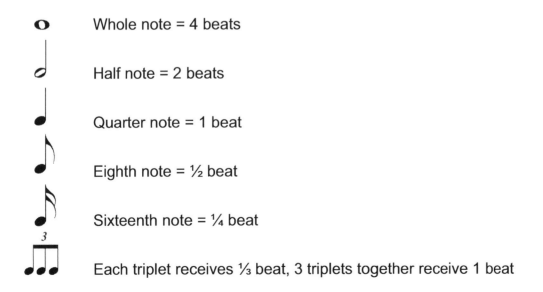

Here are examples of note values when the half note receives one beat.

Note values in 2/2 time, or ¢ time:

𝐨   Whole note = 2 beats

𝅗𝅥   Half note = 1 beat

♩   Quarter note = ½ beat

♪   Eighth note = ¼ beat

Here are examples of note values when the eighth note receives one beat.

Note values in 3/8 and 6/8 time:

𝅗𝅥.   Dotted half note = 6 beats

♩.   Dotted quarter note = 3 beats

♩   Quarter note = 2 beats

♪   Eighth note = 1 beat

𝅘𝅥𝅯   Sixteenth note = ½ beat

2. Write the number of beats each note or rest receives according to the time signatures. The first measure is done for you.

104

3. Complete the music examples by adding notes or rests so that each measure has the correct number of beats.

4. Check the correct time signature for each example.

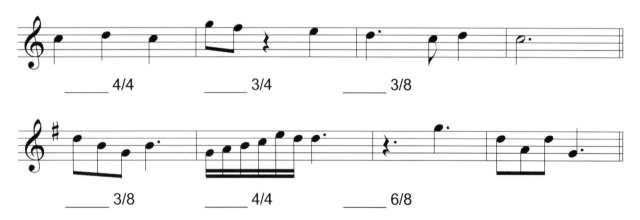

COUNTING

Here are some examples of counting. Notice that notes that receive a half beat are counted as "and", written as "+". Notes that receive a quarter beat are counted as "one e and a", written as "1 e + a". Triplets are counted as "1 trip let". Clap and count each line for rhythm practice!

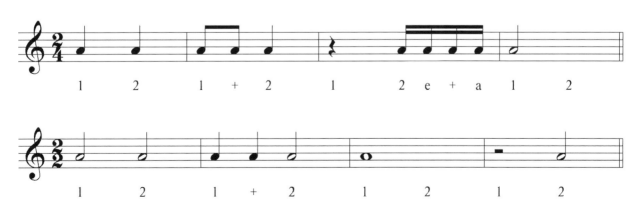

5. Write the counts under each measure. Line the beats up evenly under the notes and rests as in the examples. Clap and count each line for rhythm practice!

CHAPTER 18
Signs and Terms

Here are some common music terms and definitions:

accel., ***accelerando***: to accelerate, gradually get faster.

vivo: lively, brisk.

cantabile: songlike, singable.

espressivo: expressively.

leggiero: lightly, delicately.

subito: suddenly.

ponticello, ***pont***.: played near the bridge.

dolce: sweetly, played near or over the fretboard.

animato: animated, with spirit.

con moto: with motion.

rallentando, ***rall***.: gradually slower.

sostenuto: sustained.

meno mosso: with less motion, slower.

piu mosso: with more motion, faster.

modulation / modulate: to change key within a piece of music. For example, a piece might begin in the key of G Major and change to D Major half way through.

transposition: the act of changing a piece of music to a different key.

meter: the pattern in which rhythm and time is organized.

parallel major and minor: keys that share the same tonic note; for example: A Major and a minor.

Here are some common music symbols:

grace note

slur

accent (played with emphasis)

trill written as ... or ...

played as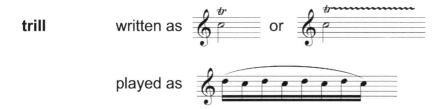

tenuto (held, sustained)

Here are some tempos that are new to Level 3:

adagio: slow; slower than andante, but not as slow as largo

largo: very slow

presto: very fast; faster than allegro

Here is a list of all the tempos we have learned in Levels 1 - 3 from **slowest** to **fastest**.

Largo   Lento   Adagio   Andante   Moderato   Allegro   Vivace   Presto

1. Check the **slower** tempo in each pair.
   ___ adagio   ___ lento
   ___ presto   ___ moderato

2. Check the **faster** tempo in each pair
   ___ largo   ___ vivace
   ___ andante   ___ allegro

3. Check the correct name for each symbol.

   ___ tenuto   ___ grace note
   ___ trill   ___ tenuto
   ___ accent   ___ slur

   ___ slur   ___ trill
   ___ accent   ___ grace note
   ___ trill   ___ slur

4. Check the correct definition for each term.

   meno mosso   ___ with less motion, slower
                     ___ lively, brisk
                     ___ expressively

   subito   ___ with more motion, faster
                     ___ suddenly
                     ___ sustained

   rallentando   ___ expressively
                     ___ animated, with spirit
                     ___ gradually slower

   leggiero   ___ with more motion, faster
                     ___ lightly, delicately
                     ___ sustained

   meter   ___ with more motion, faster
                     ___ to change key within a piece of music
                     ___ the pattern in which rhythm and time is organized

accelerando
    __ with less motion, slower
    __ to accelerate, gradually get faster
    __ gradually slower

animato
    __ suddenly
    __ animated, with spirit
    __ gradually slower

con moto
    __ with motion
    __ the pattern in which rhythm and time is organized
    __ to change key within a piece of music

cantabile
    __ songlike, singable
    __ lightly, delicately
    __ suddenly

dolce
    __ played near the bridge
    __ sweetly, played near or over the fretboard
    __ with motion

transposition
    __ the act of changing a piece of music to a different key
    __ played near the bridge
    __ animated, with spirit

ponticello
    __ sweetly, played near or over the fretboard
    __ songlike, singable
    __ played near the bridge

5. Name the **parallel minor** key for the following Major keys:

G Major: __ minor

F♯ Major: __ minor

E♭ Major: __ minor

CHAPTER 19

Music Analysis
Waltz

Answer the questions about the *Waltz* by Dionisio Aguado. Measure numbers are given above each measure.

1. How many beats are in each measure?
   __ 4   __ 3   __ 8

2. How many beats does the circled note in measure 1 receive?
   __ 1 ½ beats __ 2 beats __ 3 beats

3. How many beats does the boxed note in measure 1 receive?
__ ½ beat   __ 1 beat   __ 2 beats

4. How fast is the song to be played?
__ very slowly   __ moderately   __ fast and lively

5. How many beats does the circled note in measure 4 receive?
__ 1 beat   __ 1 ½ beats   __ 2 beats

6. How many beats does the boxed rest in measure 4 receive?
__ ½ beat   __ 1 beat   __ 3 beats

7. How many beats does the circled note receive in measure 5?
__ ¼ beat   __ ½ beat   __ 2 beats

8. What is the circled interval in measure 6?
__ P4   __ M6   __ m6

9. How many beats does the circled chord receive in measure 8?
__ 1 beat   __ 2 beats   __ 4 beats

10. What is the circled chord in measure 10?
__ b minor   __ g minor   __ G Major

11. What is the circled chord in measure 12?
__ C Major   __ c minor   __ G Major

12. What fret is the circled note played on in measure 13?
__ Fret 3   __ Fret 4   __ Fret 5

13. What fret is the circled note played on in measure 14?
__ Fret 2   __ Fret 3   __ Fret 4

14. What fret is the circled note played on in measure 15?
__ Fret 0   __ Fret 1   __ Fret 3

15. What is the circled interval in measure 21?
__ M2   __ m3   __ M3

16. What is the circled interval in measure 28?
__ m6   __ M7   __ P8

17. What key is this piece in?
__ C Major   __ A Major   __ D Major

LEVEL THREE

Final Exam

1. Write the note name and fret number below each note.

Notes on the **first string**

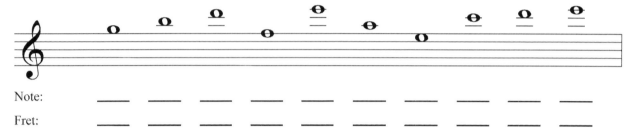

Note: ___ ___ ___ ___ ___ ___ ___ ___ ___
Fret: ___ ___ ___ ___ ___ ___ ___ ___ ___

Notes on the **second string**

Note: ___ ___ ___ ___ ___ ___ ___ ___ ___
Fret: ___ ___ ___ ___ ___ ___ ___ ___ ___

Notes on the **third string**

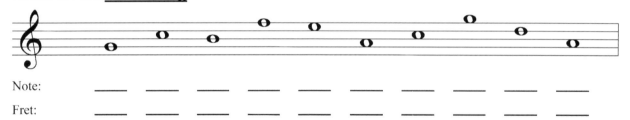

Note: ___ ___ ___ ___ ___ ___ ___ ___ ___
Fret: ___ ___ ___ ___ ___ ___ ___ ___ ___

Notes on the **fourth string**

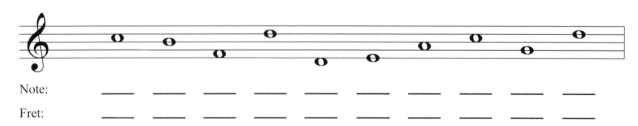

Note: ___ ___ ___ ___ ___ ___ ___ ___ ___
Fret: ___ ___ ___ ___ ___ ___ ___ ___ ___

Notes on the **fifth string**

Note: ___ ___ ___ ___ ___ ___ ___ ___ ___

Fret: ___ ___ ___ ___ ___ ___ ___ ___ ___

Notes on the **sixth string**

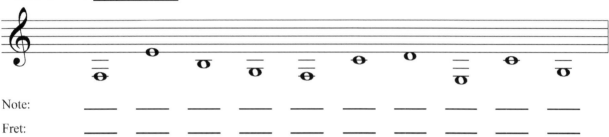

Note: ___ ___ ___ ___ ___ ___ ___ ___ ___

Fret: ___ ___ ___ ___ ___ ___ ___ ___ ___

2. Name the notes below.

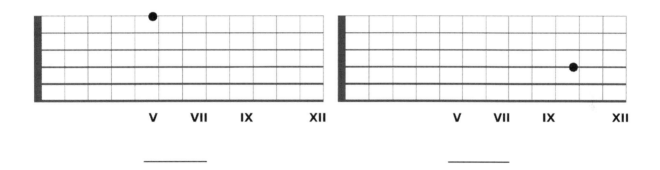

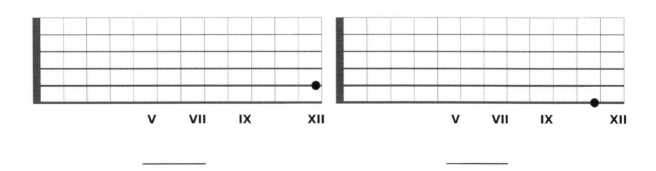

117

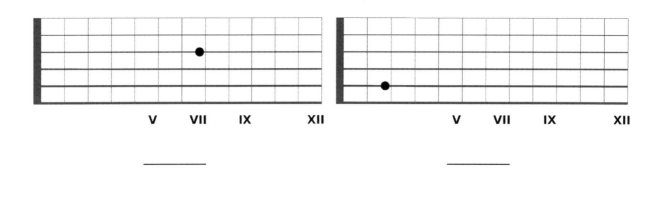
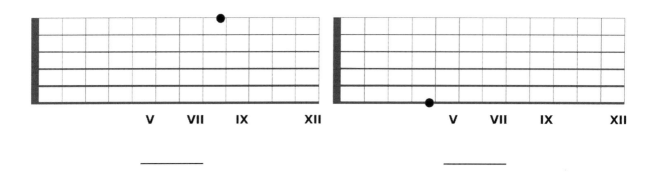
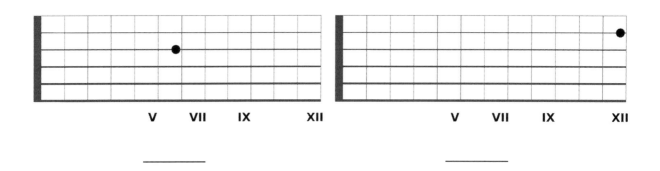
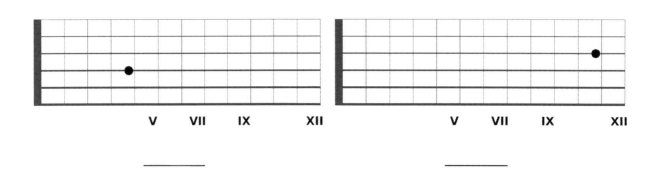

3. Draw the notes to create the **Major scales**. Draw one-octave scales and draw all **whole notes**.

G Major

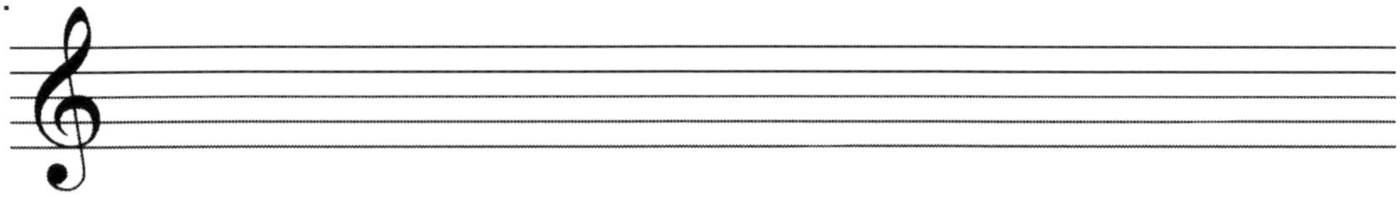

A Major

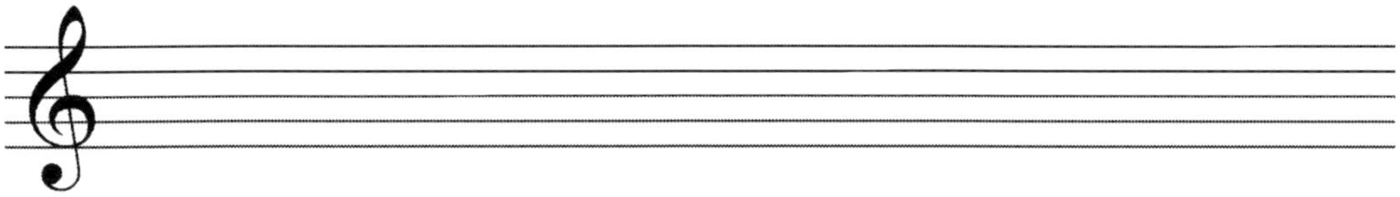

F♯ Major

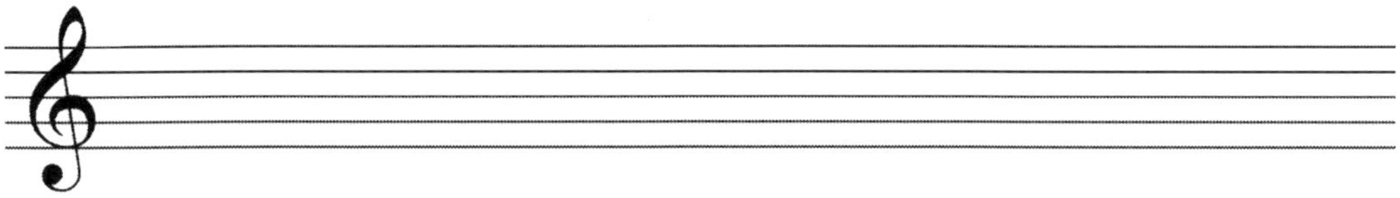

D Major

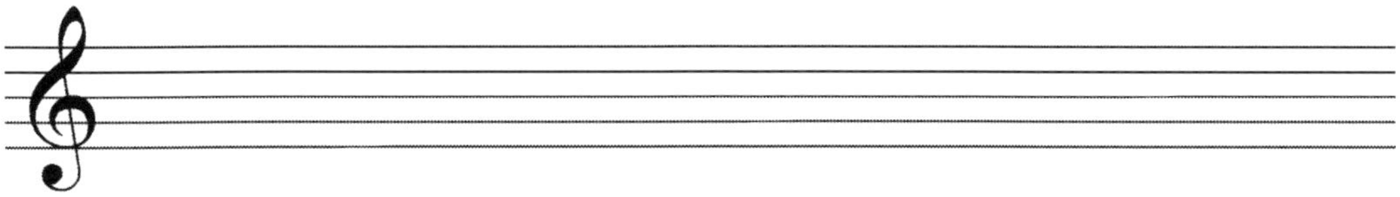

E Major

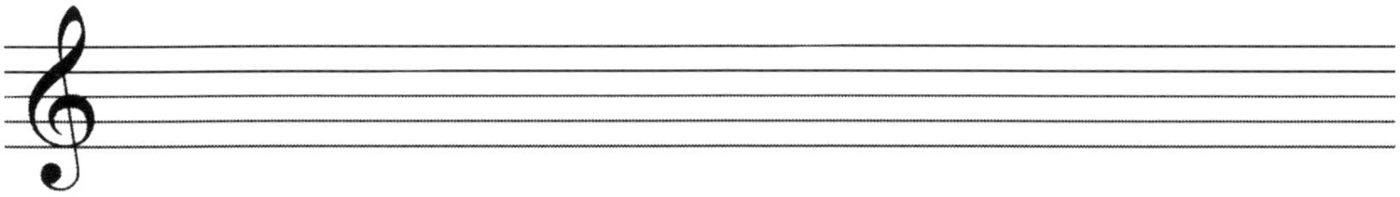

F Major

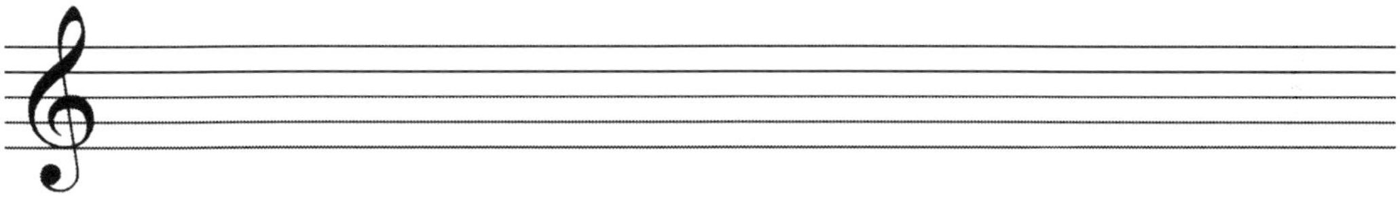

B♭ Major

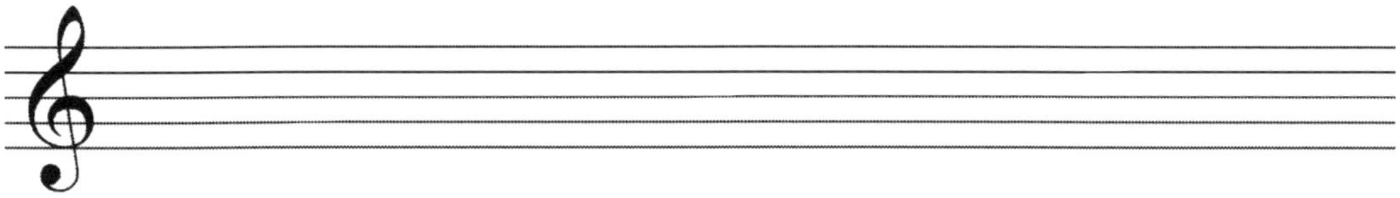

D♭ Major

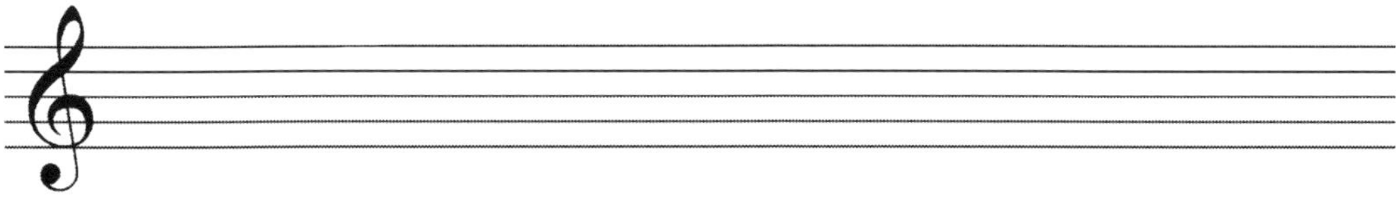

E♭ Major

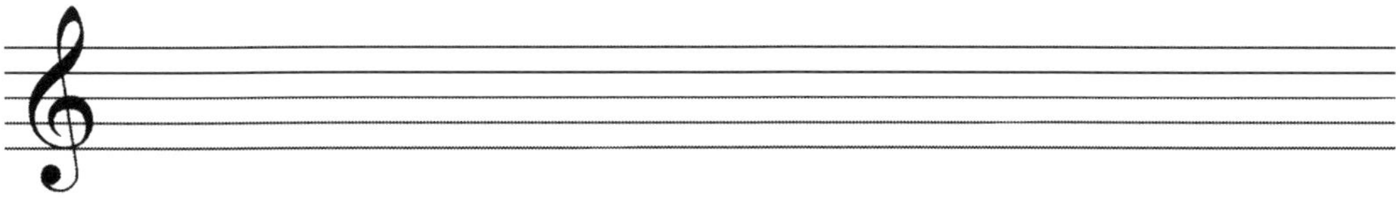

4. Name the Major and minor key for each key signature.

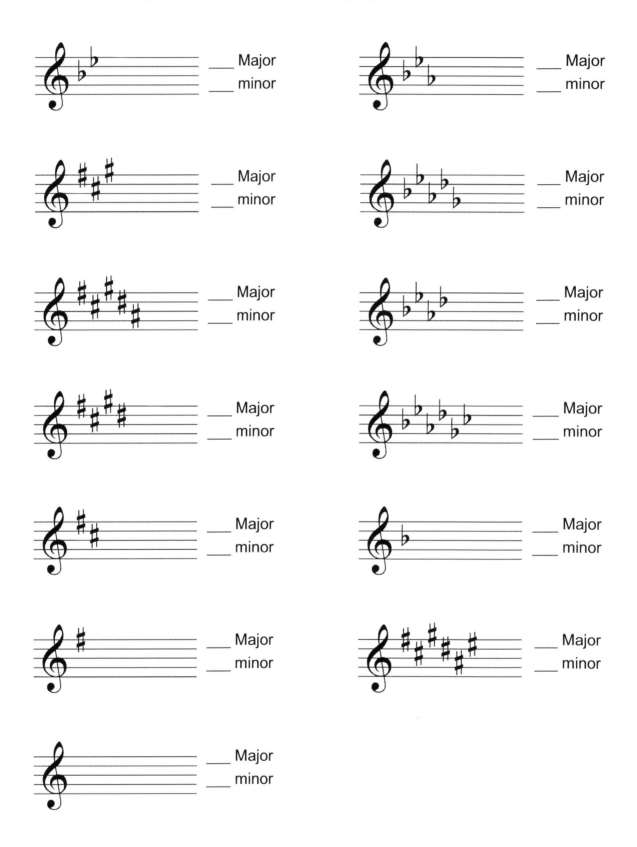

5. Write the order of **flats**: ___ ___ ___ ___ ___ ___ ___

6. Write the order of **sharps**: ___ ___ ___ ___ ___ ___ ___

7. Draw the notes to create the **minor scales**. Draw one-octave scales and draw all **half notes**. Melodic minor scales should be written ascending and descending.

b harmonic minor

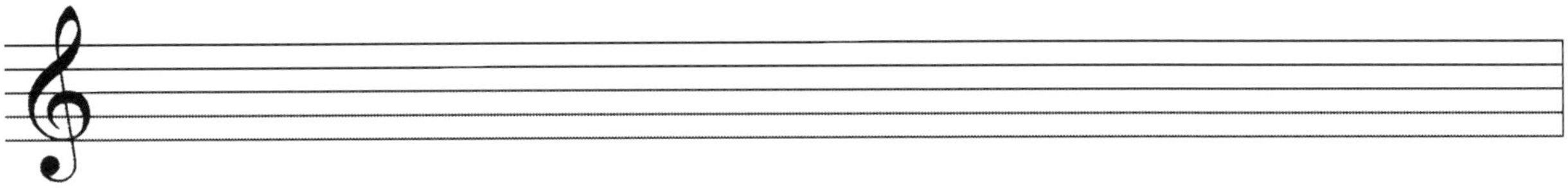

a melodic minor

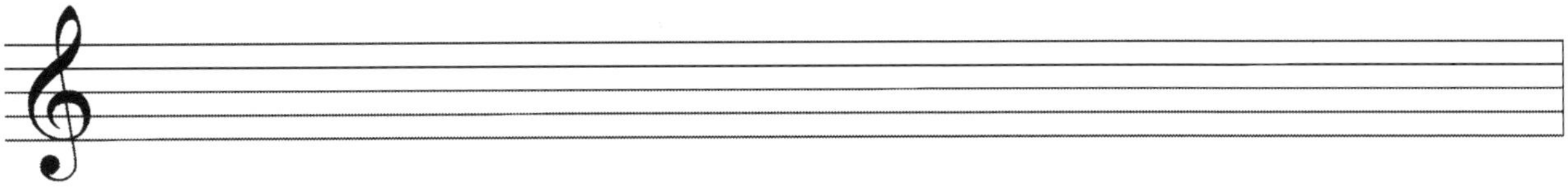

g natural minor

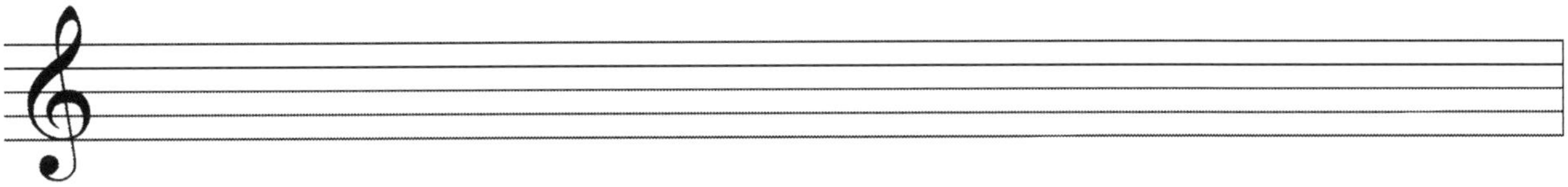

f# natural minor

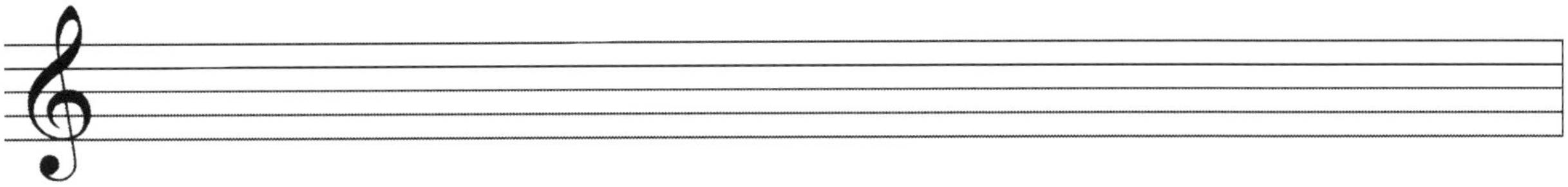

d melodic minor

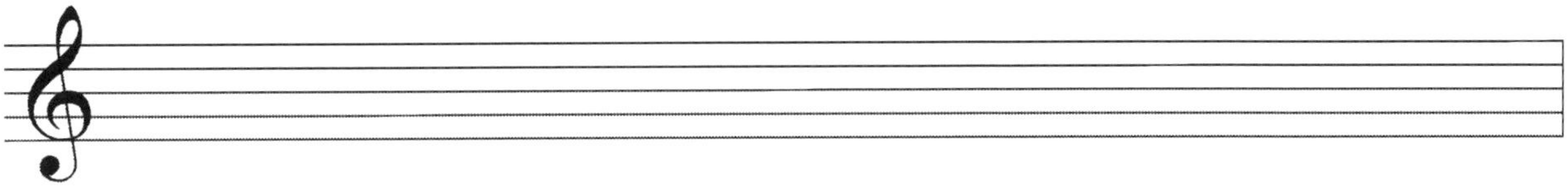

c# harmonic minor

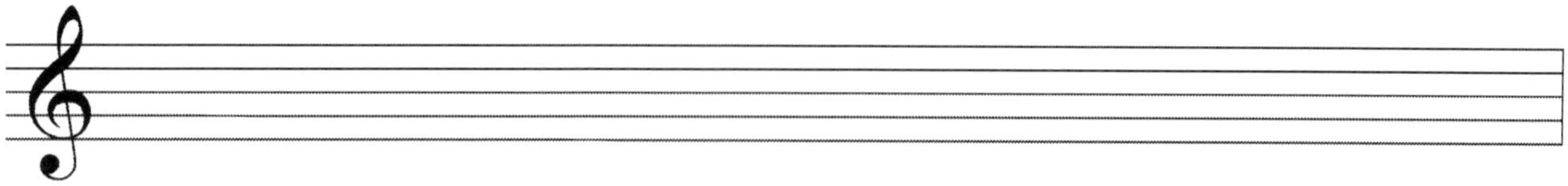

c melodic minor

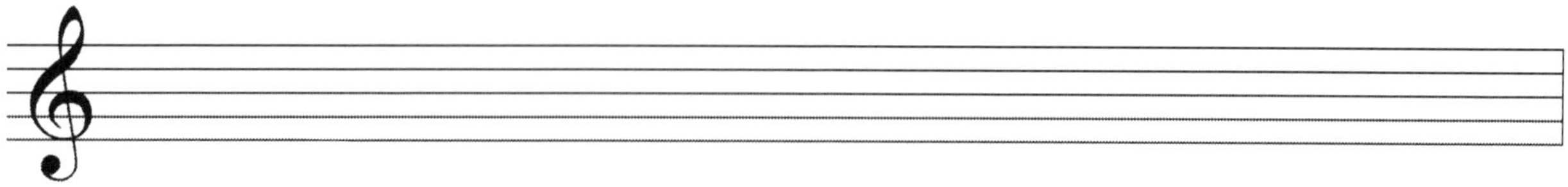

e harmonic minor

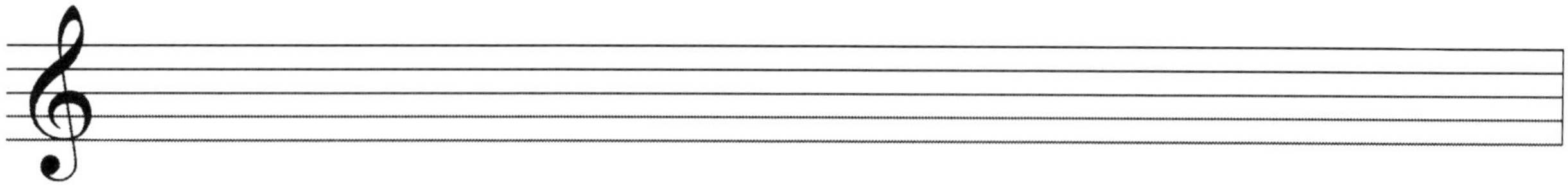

f natural minor

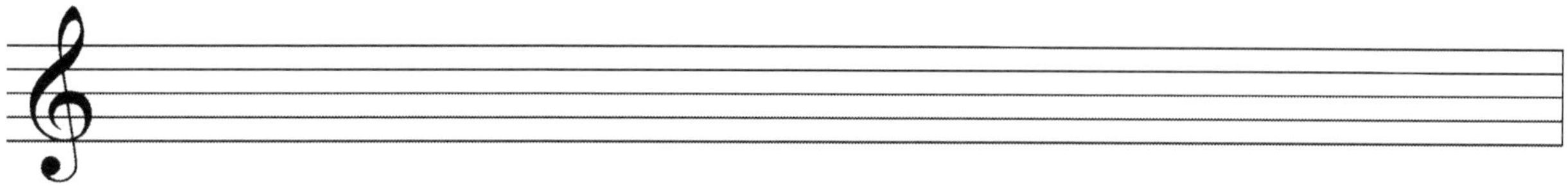

g# natural minor

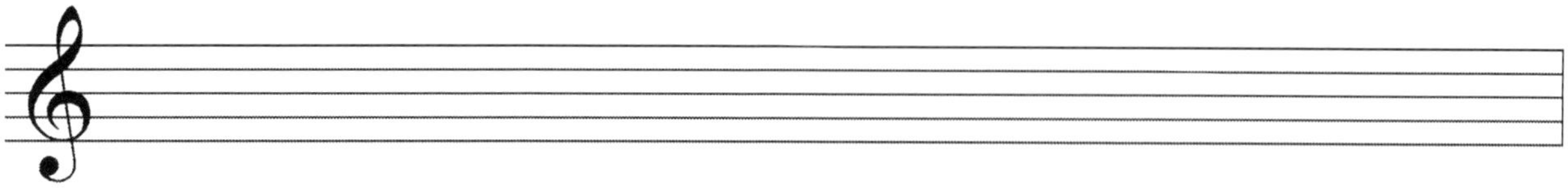

b♭ melodic minor

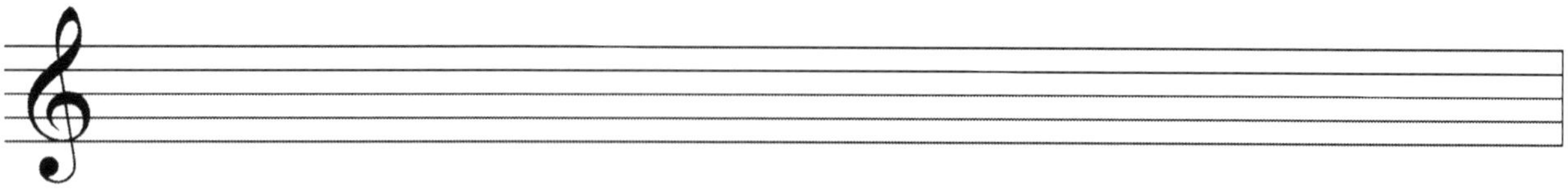

8. Complete the circle of fifths by adding the following:
    Major keys
    Minor keys
    Key signatures

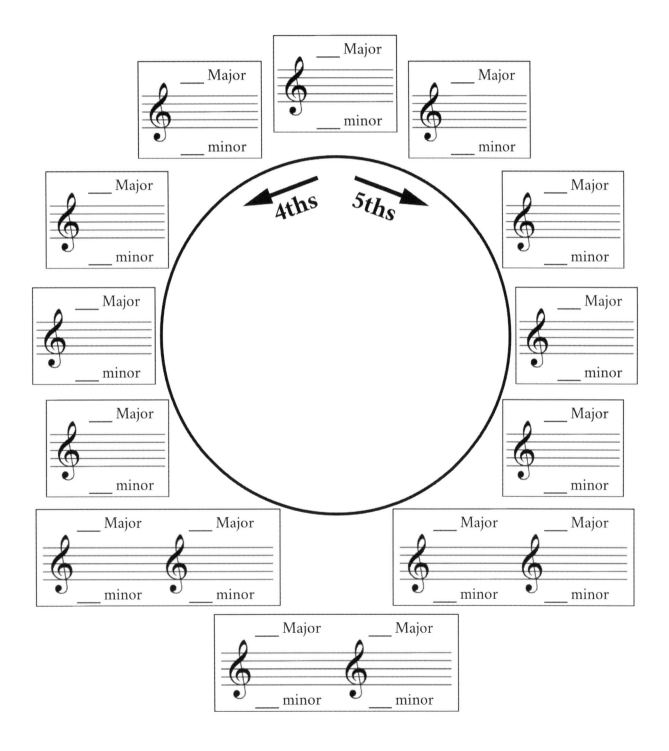

9. Draw the **upper** note to create the intervals. Draw all **whole notes** to create harmonic intervals and include sharp or flat signs when needed.

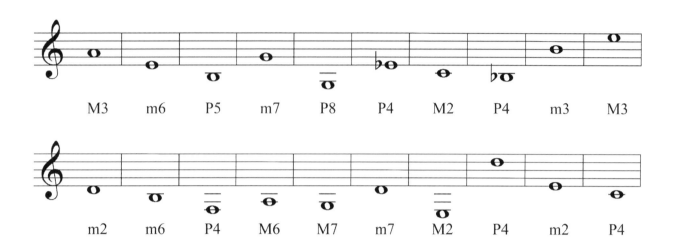

10. Name the intervals. They can be Perfect, Major, or minor. Use capital **P** for Perfect, capital **M** for Major, and lowercase **m** for minor (for example, P5, M3, m7).

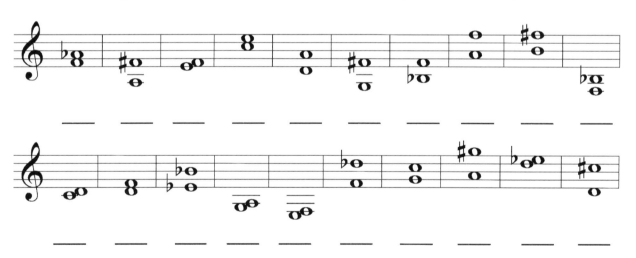

124

11. Draw the **upper two notes** above each root note to complete the **Major triads** and write the name of the triad on the line under the staff. Major triads are named with UPPERCASE letters. Include sharp or flat signs when needed.

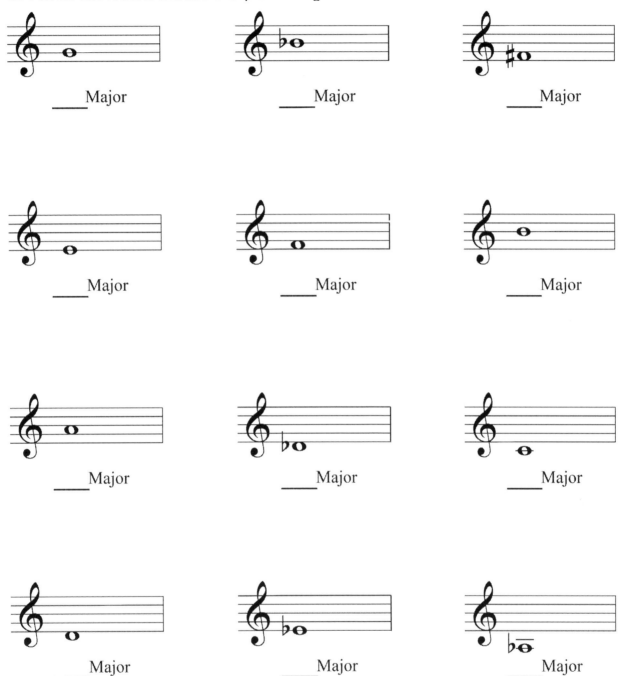

125

12. Draw the **upper two notes** above each root note to complete the **minor triads** and write the name of the triad on the line under the staff. Minor triads are named with lowercase letters. Include sharp or flat signs when needed.

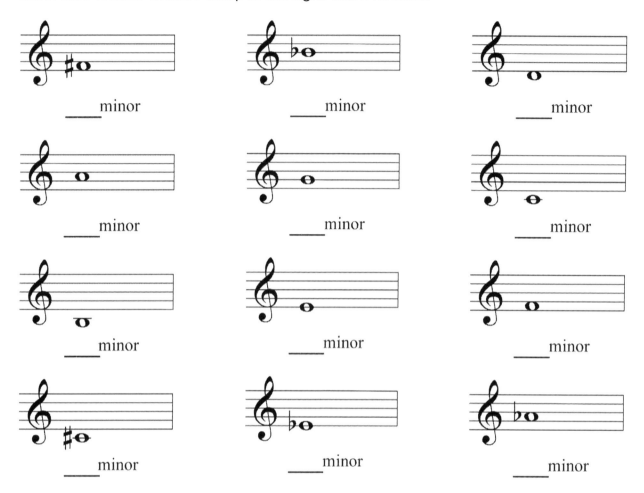

13. Name the chords. They can be Major, minor, or Dominant 7 chords. Include the letter name and chord quality (for example, G Major, d minor, B7, etc.).

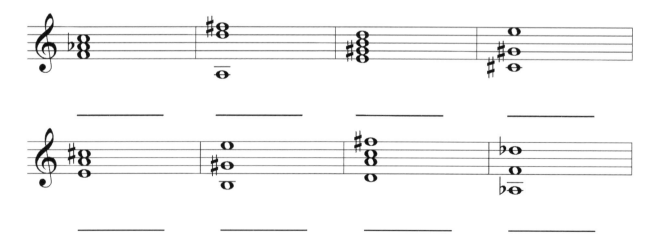

126

14. Name the barre chords. They can be Major, minor, or Dominant 7 chords.

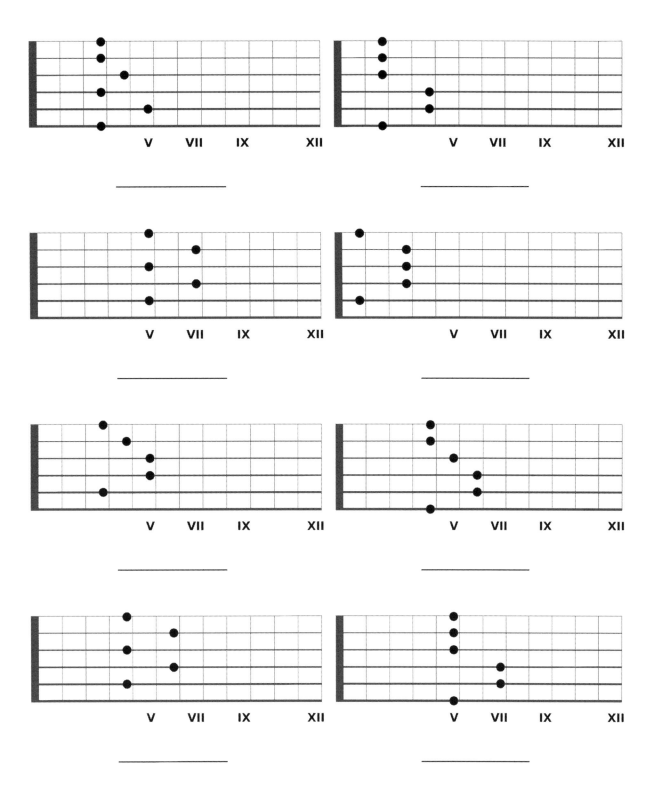

15. Draw chords to create each cadence. Follow the given key signatures.

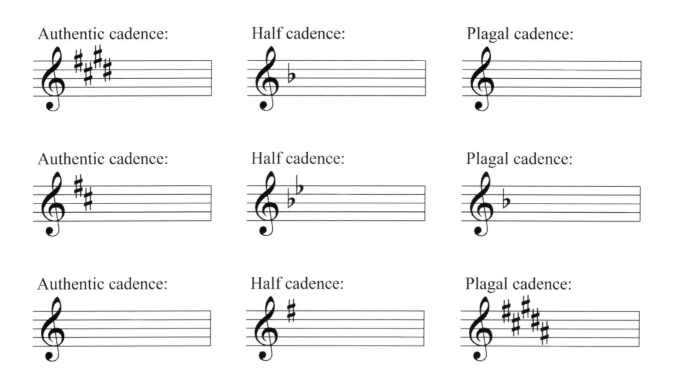

16. Write the Roman numerals and chord names under each chord progression. Follow the key signatures.

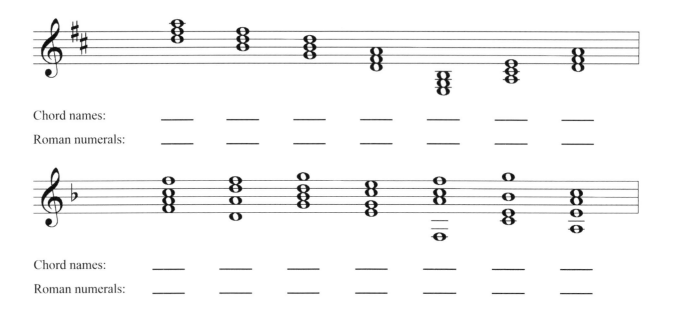

Chord names:

Roman numerals:

Chord names:

Roman numerals:

128

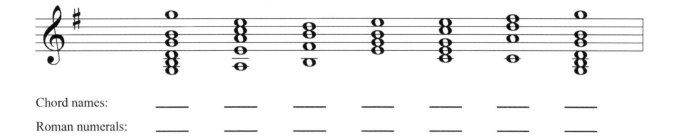

Chord names: ___ ___ ___ ___ ___ ___ ___

Roman numerals: ___ ___ ___ ___ ___ ___ ___

17. Write **chord scales** for the following Major keys. Draw **triads**. Draw sharp or flat signs next to the notes when needed (do not include key signatures). Write the Roman numerals under each chord. The first triad of each key is done for you.

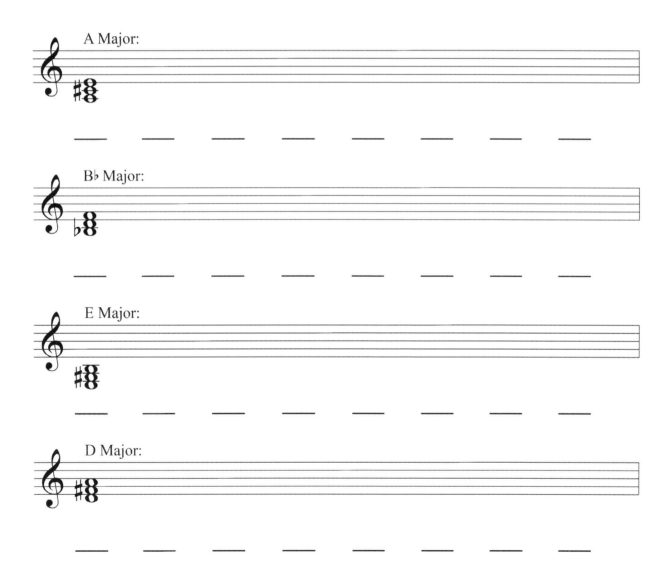

129

18. Write the Roman numerals under each chord progression and transpose them to the given keys.

Key of C Major: C   em   am   F   C   G   C

Roman numerals: ___   ___   ___   ___   ___   ___   ___

Transpose to the
key of F Major: ___   ___   ___   ___   ___   ___   ___

Key of G Major: G   D   am   C   G   D7   G

Roman numerals: ___   ___   ___   ___   ___   ___   ___

Transpose to the
key of E Major: ___   ___   ___   ___   ___   ___   ___

19. Transpose the following melody.

Key of C Major:

Transpose **down** to the key of A Major:

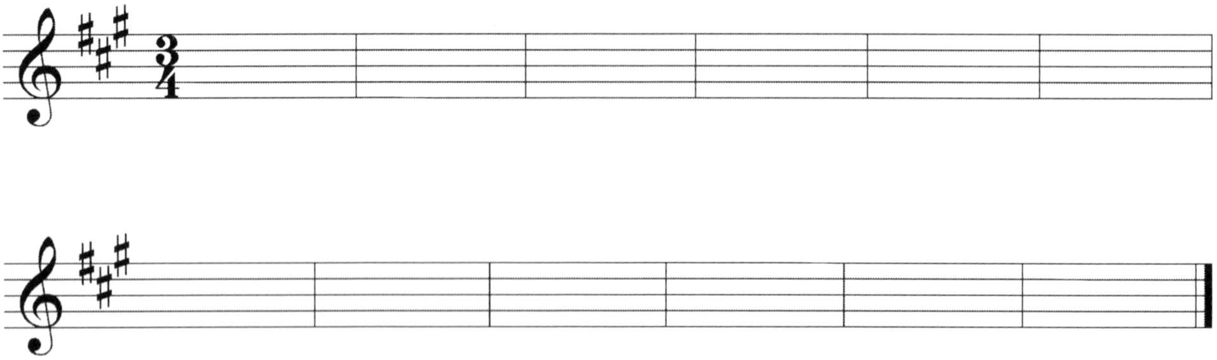

130

20. Check the correct name of each note or rest.

♪ ___ eighth note
   ___ sixteenth note
   ___ whole note

▬ ___ whole rest
   ___ half rest
   ___ quarter rest

𝄼· ___ dotted half rest
    ___ dotted eighth rest
    ___ dotted quarter rest

♩ ___ half note
   ___ quarter note
   ___ eighth note

𝄽 ___ quarter rest
   ___ eighth rest
   ___ sixteenth rest

o ___ whole note
   ___ half note
   ___ quarter note

21. Write the number of beats each note or rest receives in **4/4** time under the notes and rests.

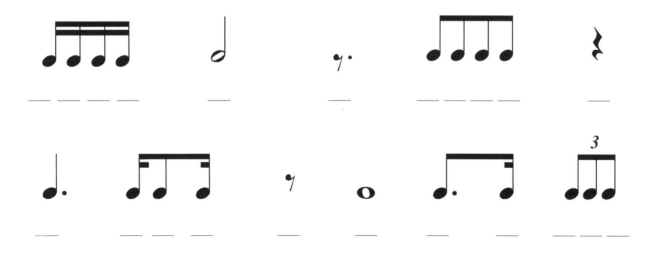

22. Write the number of beats each note or rest receives in **6/8** time under the notes and rests.

23. Check the correct time signature for each example.

___ 2/4 ___ 3/4 ___ 4/4

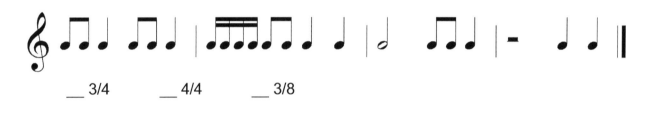

___ 3/4 ___ 4/4 ___ 3/8

___ 6/8 ___ 3/8 ___ 4/4

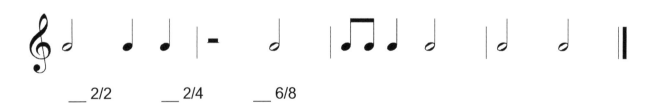

___ 2/2 ___ 2/4 ___ 6/8

24. Write the **counts** under each measure. Line the beats up evenly under the notes and rests.

25. Check the fastest tempo in each group.

___ Allegro   ___ Largo   ___ Adagio

___ Lento   ___ Vivace   ___ Andante

___ Presto   ___ Moderato   ___ Adagio

26. Check the correct definition for each term.

leggiero
　　__ suddenly
　　__ animated
　　__ lightly, delicately

sostenuto
　　__ gradually slower
　　__ lively, brisk
　　__ sustained

rallentando
　　__ gradually slower
　　__ expressively
　　__ songlike, singable

Answer the questions about the *Rondo* by Matteo Carcassi. Measure numbers are given above each measure.

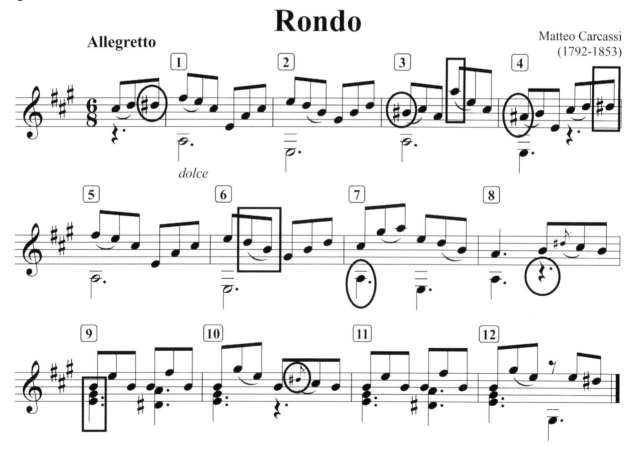

27. How many beats are in each measure?
   ___ 3   ___ 6   ___ 8

28. What is the key?
   ___ C Major   ___ E Major   ___ A Major

29. How is measure 1 to be played?
   ___ sweetly   ___ quietly   ___ suddenly

30. What fret is the circled note in measure 3 played on?
   ___ fret 0   ___ fret 1   ___ fret 3

31. What fret is the boxed note in measure 3 played on?
   ___ fret 3   ___ fret 4   ___ fret 5

32. What fret is the circled note in measure 4 played on?
   ___ fret 1   ___ fret 2   ___ fret 3

33. What fret is the boxed note in measure 4 played on?
   ___ fret 1   ___ fret 3   ___ fret 4

34. What is the boxed symbol in measure 6 called?
   ___ slur   ___ grace note   ___ tenuto

35. How many beats does the circled note in measure 7 receive?
   ___ 1 beat   ___ 1 ½ beats   ___ 3 beats

36. How many beats does the circled rest in measure 8 receive?
   ___ 1 beat   ___ 1 ½ beats   ___ 3 beats

37. What is the boxed triad in measure 9?
   ___ G Major   ___ E Major   ___ e minor

38. What is the circled symbol in measure 10 called?
   ___ slur   ___ grace note   ___ tie

Certificate of Completion

MUSIC THEORY FOR GUITAR

Level 3

This certifies that

_____

has mastered Music Theory for Guitar, Level 3

_____   _____
instructor   on this day

More Music Publications by Amy Hite

*Publications are available on Amazon.com,
StringsByMail.com, and SheetMusicPlus.com*

Music Theory for Guitar: Levels 1, 2, and 3

A comprehensive workbook series designed to help guitarists learn all aspects of music theory. Includes lessons and written exercises.

Christmas Music for Easy Classical Guitar

A collection of 24 Christmas favorites arranged for easy classical guitar.

Easy Christmas Music for Beginner Guitar

The easiest collection of Christmas music ever for the early beginning guitarist! Includes single-note notation and tablature with chord accompaniment.

Folk Music for Easy Classical Guitar

A collection of 30 familiar folk songs arranged for easy classical guitar.

Music Note Story Speller Series

A series of workbooks designed to help young students learn to read music notes in a fun way while building educational stories.

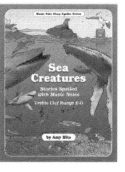

Study with Amy online! Visit **www.AmyHiteGuitar.com** for information.

Made in the USA
Las Vegas, NV
28 January 2024

85020811R00079